A
TEACHER'S
GUIDE

Andy Kempe and Rick Holroyd

imaging

A
TEACHER'S
GUIDE

Andy Kempe and Rick Holroyd

Hodder & Stoughton

A MEMBER OF THE HODDER HEADLINE GROUP

ACKNOWLEDGEMENTS

The publishers would like to thank the following for giving permission to reproduce material in this book:

p93 extract from *The Woman in Black* by Susan Hill, reproduced by permission of Penguin Books Ltd; p121 *Always a Suspect* by Mbuyiseni Oswald Mtshali, by permission of Ad. Donker (Pty) Ltd.

Every effort has been made to trace and acknowledge ownership of copyright. The publishers will be glad to make suitable arrangements with any copyright holders whom it has not been possible to contact.

British Library Cataloguing in Publication Data
A catalogue for this publication is held with the British Library

ISBN 0 340 54837 1

First published 1994
Impression number   10   9   8   7   6   5   4   3   2   1
Year   1999 1998 1997 1996 1995 1994

Copyright © 1994

Typeset by Litho Link Limited, Welshpool, Powys, Wales.
Printed in Great Britain for Hodder & Stoughton Educational –
a division of Hodder Headline plc, 338 Euston Road, London
NW1 3BH by Thomson Litho Limited, East Kilbride, Scotland.

CONTENTS

CHAPTER 1

INTRODUCTION

This series of books has arisen from a long and close collaboration between a Drama and an English teacher. As we shared ideas with each other, and often classes, we became increasingly convinced that the teaching strategies used in our different disciplines had a good deal to offer each other.

Our fundamental conviction was that Drama was no more limited to the reading and performing of scripted plays than English was to the writing of essays. Similarly, endless small group improvisations and decontextualised acting exercises could be as boring as pages of punctuation and spelling tests. We had long ago discovered that 'Drama games' were too often a distraction from the exciting work that could be done in the Drama studio, just as word games quickly wore thin in the English classroom.

We agreed that creative group work in Drama and English could promote personal, social and moral development, while the careful exploration of well-chosen resources could help develop an awareness of the historical and political context of issues. We are keen, however, to avoid over-stressing the development of what we see as essentially by-products of a practical engagement in our subjects. Our preference is more towards helping students enjoy getting better at using the disciplines for themselves. This means being able to *make* and *present* something of their own, through the use of Drama and language, and to *respond* to things expressed in those media.[1]

As we mastered more techniques and devised more strategies for our mutual use, two principles emerged which applied equally to classroom and studio:

1 The work must be *about something*. It must have *content* as well as *form.*

2 Students will be most engaged when they play a part in the direction and outcome of the work.

While we have been collecting and formulating materials for this book, the debate about the National Curriculum has developed into a debate about how it should be delivered and assessed. We have tried to assimilate and use these debates in order to present a range of resources, tasks and structures of work which are flexible but focused, pertinent but not prescriptive.

Drama and English are related, but independent of each other. Many of the strategies we use are useful in the teaching of both subjects, though the purpose for

---

1 The Arts 5–16: A Curriculum Framework *(Oliver & Boyd, 1990) offers a clear and concise argument about how different art forms relate to each other by sharing the same essential process.*

using them may be very different. The National Curriculum for English has helped provide both the criteria and the means by which Drama work may be assessed and monitored in the context of the English classroom. It is our particular intention also to use the framework provided by the Arts Council's *Drama in Schools* publication as a foundation on which to build clearly-defined, productive and progressive practice in the Drama studio. To that end, we hope this book provides a bridge between what has already been done and what is waiting to be developed in both subjects.

HOW THIS BOOK WORKS

The purpose of this book, and of the three Students' Books it accompanies, is to present a broad range of resource-inspired activities for students working towards Key Stage 3. The strategies proposed can, however, be adapted for use with small groups of top juniors whose time is flexible, as well as with Year 9 classes constrained by short, timetabled lessons.

Each of the Students' Books presents a varied mine of individual resources, clustered around particular themes under an overall heading. For example, in *Evacuees*, students are presented with materials on:

- Preparing the Hosts
- Finding Homes
- Settling In
- Problems
- School Life

Specific tasks, addressed directly to the students, indicate ways of using and developing each resource. In this way, the resources may be used as the basis for:

- individual class lessons controlled by the teacher;
- extended small group projects controlled by the students.

Each Students' Book contains ideas and materials suitable for developing into a presentation which will reflect the theme of the unit. Again, the tasks do not prescribe the exact outcome of such work but give guidance on how to select, shape and present the material.

In this Teacher's Book, notes accompanying the resources are divided into two sections:

1 Structures
  Different routes through the collected resources are described in terms of structures, designed to provide enough work for at least half a term. The key learning areas addressed in each structure are clearly stated, and moments in the work which offer different choices for development are highlighted.

2 Resources

Each task printed in the Students' Book is also registered. The purpose and organisation of many of the tasks is self-evident, and these are presented without further elaboration; for others, we pinpoint what we believe to be the chief objective and put forward particular strategies or possible further activities. Here is an example:

I Tableau[1]

Groups: 3–5[2]   10 mins[3]
Objective: To discuss the meaning of visual images.

In reviewing the tableaux, ask the class to suggest what the characters might be thinking. Is it the same as what they might be saying?[4]

---

1 *Nature of activity.*
2 *Structure of class to individual activity.*
3 *Time to be allocated.*
4 *Brief guidelines for the teacher.*

Each task will help students learn more about the resources and their implications. In this respect, the work could be said to be issue-based. However, the nature of the work and its focus on *form* empowers the students in the creative use of Drama and language rather than in the use of these disciplines as didactic tools. Our model of the system looks like this:

Creative work used to give an insight into the . . .   →   CONTENT   →   . . . used to inspire students' own creative response.

Jean-Luc Godard said:

> You can either start with fiction or with documentary. But whichever you start with, you will inevitably find the other.

It is in the interchange between the objective, unfeeling world 'out there' and the subjective, feeling world within each one of us that meanings are made, interpreted and developed into new expressions.

---

2 *The National Curriculum Council's 1991 wall chart, 'Drama in the National Curriculum', notes how role plays and technical and empathetic aspects of Drama might serve other subjects.*

 # DRAMA IN SCHOOLS

This chapter outlines the part that Drama plays in the whole school curriculum and offers criteria by which Drama may be assessed at Key Stage 3.

Drama makes four important and distinct contributions to school life:

1 It delivers other curriculum areas.
   By structuring activities in the fiction of a dramatic framework, many teachers find students are more engaged in a broad range of tasks. The dramatic nature of the work gives it an importance and urgency which may be missing from decontextualised classroom exercises.

2 It is a subject in its own right.
   Drama is a popular choice at GCSE and, increasingly, at A level. Like Art and Music, the discipline has its own distinctive history and characteristics. The relationship between theatre, literature, film and television gives the study of those characteristics a considerable importance in an increasingly dramatised world.

3 It complements work across the curriculum.
   Elements of Drama, such as role play, are often used in other subjects.[2] Some schools directly address the personal, social and moral development of students, their development of language, and issues of gender and culture, through a separate part of their timetabled curriculum. Other schools have adopted whole school policies to ensure that each subject assumes some responsibility for the delivery of this wider curriculum. Given Drama's extensive use of group work and its dialectic (rather than didactic) approach, the strategies it commonly uses have a clear role to play in either approach.

4 It provides regular or periodic performances of plays.
   Dramatic presentations might occur in assemblies, where groups share with the rest of the school the work they have been doing in class. Some performances might be to parents: these may be built from the students' own research and improvisations or rehearsed from scripts discovered and explored during the course of working on a particular theme. Dramatic performance is very much a part of the tradition of most schools. Parents, staff and, above all, children benefit from such presentations, especially when the content and theatrical possibilities of the play allow the company to stretch their talents and imaginations.[3]

We believe that there is a place for all of these contributions in both primary and

---

2 *The National Curriculum Council's 1991 wall chart, 'Drama in the National Curriculum', notes how role plays and technical and empathetic aspects of Drama might serve other subjects.*
3 *For a fuller account of the Drama culture in schools, see David Hornbrook's* Education in Drama *(Falmer Press, 1991).*

secondary schools, and the tasks proposed in this book span all four areas. However, the Drama specialist will wish to know how to encourage, monitor and record progression and achievement in Drama as a curriculum subject in its own right.[4]

DRAMATIC ACTIVITY

Exactly what the subject of Drama entails in the school curriculum can be seen to range from games to simple recitation of verse. Central to our thinking is that Drama is concerned with the relationship between *content* and *form*. Drama is always *about* something, but the way these ideas are expressed inevitably affects how they are understood.[5] In Drama, students make, perform and respond to plays. The Arts Council's *Drama in Schools* report (1992) describes the subject as follows:

> Drama is an art, a practical activity and an intellectual discipline. It involves the creation of imagined characters and situations which are enacted within a designated space. A drama education which begins with play may eventually include all the elements of theatre. Like all the arts, drama helps us to make sense of the world.

Making Drama

There is a world of difference between having an idea which would make a great play and actually being able to produce that play! In practice, students engaged in dramatic activity might be seen as working in a continuum, involving moving from the generation of ideas to fixing those ideas by using a set of conventions associated with the art form we call Drama. The continuum resembles the one that runs between a child playing in the home corner and the professional actor or playwright or director. To describe the continuum as linear, however, might be misleading. This implies a progression by age and skill from one end of the continuum to the other. Perhaps it is more accurate and more useful to see the progression as being between having an idea and being able to realise it effectively; this has less to do with age than with the guidance, advice and range of experiences offered to a student at key moments in the process of making something meaningful.[6]

---

4 Andy Kempe's article 'Odd Bed Fellows' (The Drama Magazine, 1990) argues that social, personal and moral development should be the product of all good teaching, no matter what the subject area. Drama teachers should certainly not ignore these areas but might justifiably see them as being secondary to facilitating the students' development as producers and receivers of Drama.

5 The relationship between content and form is set out in more detail in Andy Kempe's GCSE Drama Coursebook (Blackwells, 1990), and discussed further in Gavin Bolton's book, New Perspectives On Classroom Drama (Simon & Schuster, 1992).

6 See Lev Vygotsky's account of how children learn most effectively when adults actively collaborate in the learning process. An accessible summary of Vygotsky's work and how it relates to Drama may be found in David Davis's article, 'Drama, Learning and Mental Development', in 2D Magazine, Vol. 6, No. 1, 1986.

'Making Drama' involves both creative and technical elements:

1 Creative input

This activity is at that end of the continuum most concerned with a student's own ideas, insights, memories and feelings. In response to some kind of stimulation – a picture, a piece of literature or documentary material, or perhaps an idea thrown up in discussion or improvisation – the student is inspired to do something of his or her own. Sometimes, the initial enthusiasm to respond to a good stimulus is tremendously energetic; at other times, the teacher needs to encourage the students to form a new perspective on it from which they will more clearly see the material's potential.

2 Technical input

Like any other artists, Drama students who want to respond to something they find stimulating and relevant are faced with the problem of how to present what they want to do in a way that will be comprehensible to other people. They will need somehow to control and manipulate the art form within given conventions. Art forms, however, are forever mutating and developing, and we are certainly not suggesting that there are a number of specific skills or conventions that *need* to be learned before students can start to make their own dramas. We believe that, through actively engaging in dramatic activities, students start to learn what the constraints and limits of the form are and join the never-ending process of reshaping those constraints.[7]

'Making Drama' concerns the ability to generate and shape dramatic form in order to capture, express and explore meanings.

Performing Drama

Drama is a temporal art: one of the elements which distinguish it from other arts is the way it uses, and indeed exists in, time. David Hornbrook points out that Drama may have a *written text* and may be represented through an *electronic text*, but at its heart is the *performance text* which, once the moment is past, has vanished forever in that particular form.[8]

The word 'performance' has, understandably perhaps, been equated with the presentation of a scripted school play to an invited audience for some educationally questionable motives. What *we* understand the word to mean is simply the means whereby an idea is captured in some physical activity. This might imply an improvisation performed in response to a stimulus, spontaneously, to no one but

---

7 *Robert Witkin, in* The Intelligence of Feeling *(Heinemann, 1974), usefully describes, albeit in a taxing manner, the path children take from being stimulated through their primary senses to delivering a piece of art which has its own meaning as well as being a reflection of the children's initial impulse.*

8 *See* Education in Drama *by David Hornbrook (Falmer Press, 1991). The BFI's* Primary Media Education: A Curriculum Statement *(1989) is another informative and refreshingly clear document pertinent to this analysis.*

the performers themselves. If we accept that there operates, in every one of us, an 'internal audience' to our external actions,[9] then a good performer might be someone who has a finely developed sense of this internal audience *and* the ability to change their external presentations according to what it is telling them. 'Performance', in the sense that we understand it, would include:

- the work of a group which had been given time to formulate and shape a dramatic response to a stimulus which was then shared with the rest of the class;
- the action that followed a teacher saying, 'Hold it there! Show us again what you just did';
- the spontaneous dramatic play which followed a teacher entering a drama in role in order to challenge a decision that the students, also in role, had just made;
- anything developed for or presented to an audience, no matter who they might be (including the performers themselves) for whatever purpose (including both trivial entertainment and earnest exploration of an unfolding situation).[10]

'Performing Drama' involves engaging and communicating with an audience through the dramatic form. It is the physical process of imparting meaning.

To be 'good' at Drama does not just involve performance in terms of acting. Many Drama teachers' discomfort about the primacy of the school play has arisen because they know that there is more to Drama than tutoring acting skills. Deference must be paid to those who have the ideas and ability somehow to get others to realise these ideas even if they personally cannot. Shakespeare's own acting ability pales into insignificance when compared with his ability to impart meaning through the written word and through his understanding of the effect those words will have on an audience. And who cares whether Peter Brook or Peter Hall or any other acclaimed director can act or not? Their contribution to Drama is of a different order, but it clearly has a place in the process of making and imparting meaning. In the same way, the child who offers a new insight into the content being investigated, or who visualises an effective way of expressing an idea through the dramatic form, is a valuable asset in the Drama classroom and deserves recognition.

Responding to Drama

At its simplest level, responding to a piece of drama might involve being purely reactive: 'I liked it', 'I didn't like it'. A teacher might reasonably try to wheedle a more cognitive response by asking the student to:

- describe the content ('It was about the War');
- comment on the quality of the realisation ('I couldn't hear what she said').

---

9 Gavin Bolton's Towards a Theory of Drama in Education *(Longman, 1979) offers an introduction to the notion of the 'internal' audience that has since been developed by many other commentators.*

10 *Stephen Lacey and Brian Woolland argue that the interaction that occurs between actor and spectator in the Drama classroom is a form of theatre practice in its own right, a view which we do not think is contrary to the Arts Council model. See* New Theatre Quarterly, *Vol. 8, No. 29, Feb. 1992, 'Educational Drama and Radical Theatre Practice'.*

In order for students to improve the quality of their own work and to extrapolate more meaning from other people's, they need to develop their ability to move from a purely 'felt' response to a consciously critical one. A meaningful evaluation will consider both the content of the work ('It was about the War') and the form chosen to express it ('It relied on spoken dialogue'). This means understanding both what a good idea looks like and what an appropriate way to communicate it would be. Furthermore, a consideration of *how* it has been expressed will affect the way its meaning is understood.

That sort of critical appreciation can only be done in a context. In other words, it becomes comparatively easy to recognise a worthy or original idea when you have come across a number of facile or clichéd ones. To make a productive judgement though, a knowledge of the form's conventions becomes imperative: how else can you know which practical techniques an audience (whoever they might be) are likely to respond positively to? Frustrating as it may be, it is at this point that we recognise the limitations of most teachers (and certainly our own) to deal effectively with dramatic forms outside of the Euro-centric tradition.[11]

Closely related to this kind of *critical* context is a broader historical and social one that we might describe as a *cultural* context. Simply knowing when Shakespeare lived does not, in itself, help students understand his plays or how they work any better. Knowing something about what life was like at the time might. What we know of the historical and social context within which a piece of art has been made, and how aware we are of the context in which it is being experienced, will affect the way we judge that text's effect and potential. Decisions about the best space, lighting and costume depend on this kind of judgement. This point is pertinent not only when considering how to stage the next school play, but also when a group is working on the propaganda of World War Two or discussing what guides the image-makers behind the modern political party conference.

In another sense, the teacher must be aware of the cultural context of the classroom itself. Teachers will want to be sensitive to the effect of materials and strategies on their own particular students. Choices will rely on an appreciation of the students as individuals and the cultural context in which they live. The accepted importance of 'knowing where the students have come from, and where they are' suggests that the students' work should be appraised *culturally* as well as *critically*.

'Responding to Drama' involves the ability to make informed and discerning judgements about Drama and to interpret, reflect on and evaluate Drama at all

---

11 *Anthropological studies, such as Clifford Geertz's* The Interpretation of Cultures *(Basic Books, New York, 1973), remind us that we can't help but understand other cultures through the medium of our own. 'Art' is not a word that occurs in every language; this could indicate that some cultures have no concept of 'art'. Conversely, the art of other cultures is sometimes bound so closely to formal convention (the Kabuki, for example) as to be explicitly a language in its own right. To encourage a sharing of and respect for the celebrations and expressions of other cultures is possible and positive, but to suggest that anyone can transcend their own cultural shackles, and so wholly comprehend them, seems to us naïve and arrogant.*

points in the process of making and performing it. It involves extracting meaning on a personal level and recognising the cultural context of one's own understanding.

If students are to take control of their own creative work, they will need to understand both the critical and the cultural context within which they work. In turn, their informed responses will stimulate the making and performing of new dramas.

RECORDING ACHIEVEMENT IN DRAMA

To be 'good' at Drama is to be good at making, performing and responding to Drama.

There are no official Attainment Targets in Drama. However, the statements below (synthesised from David Hornbrook's book, *Education in Drama*, and the Arts Council's report, *Drama in Schools*) will help the Drama teacher note the level of attainment which might be expected by the end of Key Stage 3 in these three elements. They are offered here, along with examples of what they might look like in practice, as a basis on which teachers may build their own bank of comments from which termly reports might be written.

Making Drama

Statement of Attainment	**Example**
The student has:	
(a) contributed ideas about the content and form of the work and developed them through appropriate discussion and rehearsal.	*The student verbalises some personal ideas and shows willingness to adapt them in the light of comment.*
(b) tried to use a variety of dramatic forms to communicate an idea effectively.	*Mime, tableaux, narration and flashback are experimented with as ways of making a wartime propaganda film.*
(c) used a range of stimuli as the basis for Drama related work.	*A South African police statement is read in character; a design for the character's costume is drawn in the working notebook.*
(d) found appropriate ways of recording his/her dramatic ideas.	*A student's ideas for a drama are sketched as a storyboard: a group develops the idea, and one member records the improvised drama as a script.*

(*e*) organised, dressed and lit a dramatic space effectively and used appropriate sound effects and props to convey meaning.

A student sketches a simple set to represent a railway station: others place a character on some chairs in a single spotlight to capture the loneliness of the last evacuee to find a home. One student makes a sound recording of an air-raid as the backing for a scene.

Performing Drama

Statement of Attainment

The student has:

Example

(*a*) shown some ability to sustain a dramatic role.

A student portrays a harassed teacher with conviction while being hot-seated; he/she doesn't giggle and answers questions appropriately.

(*b*) employed vocal and movement skills to portray a number of different characters.

In one scene, a student switches from narrating a story to being a character in the story.

(*c*) shown a practical understanding of the importance of space and timing in a drama.

A group carefully positions an audience as if they are witnesses to a public hanging; the students freeze the scene at the moment the hangman touches the lever.

(*d*) adapted his/her performance to suit different material and shown some ability in a variety of dramatic techniques.

One week, a student has sensitively delivered a condemned man's last speech; later, he/she displays comic timing in a scene where the man is rescued from the gallows by his loved one.

(*e*) demonstrated some knowledge of the technical aspects of presenting a drama.

A group has formulated its own documentary about Apartheid; one member effectively stage-manages the presentation which involves using sound recording and showing some slides.

Responding to Drama

Statement of Attainment

The student has:

Example

(*a*) contributed to discussions and considered other opinions about the nature of the work in hand.

A student explains his/her aims for a piece of drama and tries to understand why others found it difficult to follow.

(b) identified the different elements which make up a drama.

In his/her notebook, one student describes how he/she felt a good storyline was let down by the absence of appropriate settings.

(c) discussed different styles of dramatic presentation and seen them in a broad cultural and historical context.

One group identifies the punchy style of a wartime propaganda film as seeming humorous now: it compares it with the matter-of-fact presentation of modern newsreaders. Another group considers why there seem to be few plays about Apartheid actually written by black South Africans.

(d) demonstrated an understanding of the roles different people have in a dramatic presentation.

A group preparing a polished improvisation divides up responsibilities, such as finding pieces of costume, designing a simple set and recording a piece of music needed at the end. The group describes to the teacher informally how and why it did this.

(e) shown some understanding of how Drama relates to the other arts.

In a group discussion about life in eighteenth-century England, the students describe how important period music might be in order to set the scene.

Project Evaluation

Many Drama teachers find it useful to keep a record of a group's response to a unit of work. The record identifies those areas of Drama covered most fully by the unit and the readiness of the group to engage with them. Future work can then be geared towards addressing other areas, while the teacher can ensure that the pitch of the work is appropriate to their students' age and experience.

The profile on the next page is a model for adaptation by individual teachers:

UNIT EVALUATION

Group: _____   Term: _____   Year: _____

(tick as appropriate)

1 CONTENT

Resource Unit Title:

Brief description of main strategies or structure used:

Initial reaction to the success of the project:
  Excellent ☐
  Very good ☐
  Good ☐
  Not very good ☐
  Poor ☐

Assessment of students' reception of project:
  Enthusiastic ☐
  Interested ☐
  Accepting ☐
  Unenthusiastic ☐
  Hostile ☐

2 LEARNING OPPORTUNITIES

(ring as appropriate)

Extent to which you felt the work has helped develop:

Creativity	1	2	3	4	5
Technical skills	1	2	3	4	5
Performance skills	1	2	3	4	5
Critical response	1	2	3	4	5

Response towards:

thematic content	1	2	3	4	5
dramatic forms	1	2	3	4	5

Extent to which work promoted:

Social development of group	1	2	3	4	5
Personal skills	1	2	3	4	5
Consideration of issues	1	2	3	4	5

3 PERSONAL ASSESSMENT

What problems were there with the organisation and management of the project?

Notes on successful elements of planning and presentation:

Notes on successful/unsuccessful resources and strategies:

CHAPTER 3: DRAMA AND ENGLISH

In this chapter, the contribution Drama strategies may make to the English National Curriculum is discussed.

In Chapter Eight of the National Curriculum English document *English for ages 5–16* (1989), the valuable relationship between Drama and English is clearly outlined. Drama is advocated both as a subject in its own right (in which students will be introduced to dramatic texts and the art of the theatre) as well as a method (in which students will be encouraged to develop skills in interpretation of meaning and communicating that interpretation to an audience).

While it is most likely that the English teacher would look to the processes of Drama to complement their methodology, it is important not to overlook the importance of Drama's subject-specific content. Drama is an academic discipline in its own right: it embraces the art of theatre and a body of knowledge and theory which is quite distinct as an academic discipline from that of English. The argument that as Drama is only part of English in terms of utilising its process and it therefore may be subsumed by the latter under curriculum rationalisation, wholly ignores the importance of Drama as a distinct subject.

However, the processes involved in Drama do offer a valuable methodology to the English teacher, and can be implemented just as easily in the English classroom as well as in the Drama studio. Most obviously, the possibilities which Drama offer for developing students' language skills are clearly highlighted. Paragraph 8.11 of *English for ages 5–16* states that:

'. . . drama activities can be structured to focus pupils' energies on experimenting with and developing control of a wide variety of language styles. Drama quickly reveals to children the effectiveness of language, building up their language resources and allowing them to develop an awareness of a whole range of linguistic choices and registers. Different situations demand different emotional and linguistic responses.'

The value of Drama to the English teacher is evident in this statement. It is the construction of these 'different situations' – different contexts or different worlds – which is the key to facilitating committed spoken or written responses. The deeper the commitment to the 'different situation', the deeper the quality of the response.

In Chapter 2 the statement was made that Drama is concerned with the relationship between content and form. Similarly, the best practice in English is characterised by work which is clearly about something (its *content*) and which has a clear sense of audience (challenging students to consider the *form* of their response). It is a fairly uncontentious claim for English teaching that, when talk precedes writing, the value of the writing is enhanced. It is the nature and quality of that talk which is of importance. A class discussion to brainstorm ideas, or a five-minute talk in pairs to generate and share thoughts is fine in terms of the ideas – or *content* – it may produce, but it will not necessarily help the student to find the right mode or register – the *form* – of language to respond in. In role work, Hot-Seating and Improvisation *will* provide students with a context in which language must be used with a clear sense of audience. Such techniques will allow students to experiment with registers and vocabulary in order to find the most suitable mode of language for that context. The writing-in-role or speaking which results may well be of a higher quality if the commitment to the 'different situation' has been established.

The National Curriculum English document goes on to suggest some opportunities which Drama provides for the student in order to develop skills with language. These are given as opportunities to:

- provide information, give instructions and explanations;
- predict and plan;
- narrate, recount or report on a past or present experience, real or imagined;
- argue, discuss, defend and justify a point of view;
- persuade, negotiate or mediate;
- come to conclusions or sum up.

(*English for ages 5–16*, §8.11)

While all these activities will be commonplace in English teachers' Speaking and Listening lessons, it is our belief that the dramatic techniques used in this book will deepen the commitment to such work in the following ways:

- the tasks give ownership of the work to the students and therefore deepen their commitment to it;
- the tasks build a detailed context in which the work takes place, giving a greater sense of purpose and audience;
- the tasks demand a range of forms in which students are to respond, and the context in which the work is set allows them to experiment with different forms with increased confidence.

The English document celebrates the best work in English as being 'vigorous, committed, honest and interesting'. If teachers are to succeed in helping their students to produce work which reflects these qualities, then they must provide real contexts in which students can work. The best examples of practice in English already reflect such a methodology: the worst still reflect lessons in which students are asked to use language in 'one off' disembodied tasks which have no clear purpose or context. In such cases, the responses of the students will lack vigour, commitment, honesty and interest.

The work proposed in this book draws from the repertoire of dramatic techniques to deepen the context for writing and speaking. The tasks are intended to provide students with the opportunities to show an understanding of the content of the work, as well as illustrating their ability to write or to speak in a variety of forms, depending upon the implied audience and purpose. The following examples from the Students' Books have been presented to illustrate this range.

If Drama can provide the English teacher with the techniques to facilitate work of this kind, then it is a powerful tool with which to work. Rather than being seen as merely an adjunct of the English curriculum, it is our belief that Drama provides the English teacher with a valuable methodology in its own right which can be employed in the English classroom to promote work which is always 'vigorous, committed, honest and interesting'.

SPEAKING AND LISTENING

ATTAINMENT TARGET 1
The development of pupils' understanding of the spoken word and the capacity to express themselves effectively in a variety of speaking and listening activities, matching style and response to audience and purpose.

- A student in role as a new teacher explains to the headteacher of a township school in South Africa why he or she wants to work there.
- Some students adopt the positions of a group of evacuees in a photograph. Classmates suggest captions which convey the atmosphere of the picture.
- In role as a journalist recently returned from South Africa, a student is debriefed of his or her experiences by classmates playing the newspaper's editorial board.
- Using words from an eighteenth-century 'Canting Dictionary', students improvise a courtroom scene to explore the differences between Standard and Non-Standard forms of English and the attitudes associated with them.

READING

ATTAINMENT TARGET 2
The development of the ability to read, understand and respond to all types of writing, as well as the development of information-retrieval strategies for the purpose of study.

- Students read an extract from a novel on South Africa silently before hot-seating one of the book's characters to explore and develop the fiction.
- The class read a poem reportedly written by an evacuee and inspect it for evidence of authenticity.
- Groups compare a private letter with a newspaper report focusing on a miners' strike in South Africa, in an attempt to distinguish fact from fiction.
- Groups take a short section of Alfred Noyes' poem 'The Highwayman' and experiment with ways of reading it aloud to capture its rhythm, meaning and atmosphere.

WRITING

ATTAINMENT TARGET 3
A growing ability to construct and convey meaning in written language matching style to audience and purpose.

- In role as a teacher accompanying a group of evacuees, students write a report for the education authority on a child who has run away from his or her hosts.
- Using the opening of the folk tale 'Unana and the Elephant', the students use prediction and knowledge of previous reading in the genre to write their own version.
- Using the evidence given on housing in South Africa, the students, in role as estate agents, draw up a detailed description of a fictional white character's home.
- Students write the farewell speech a popular highwayman might have delivered to his admirers from the gallows.

CHAPTER 4: TOOLS FOR THE TEACHER

This chapter explains the strategies and teaching techniques used to explore and develop the resources in the Students' Books and demonstrates the relevance of standard classroom practice.

Many of the terms used in books on Drama in education can seem imprecise. With some terms such as 'improvisation', this is understandable. However, some can be confusing and intimidating to teachers new to them, if the terms are not defined and qualified. The notes below describe how we understand and employ certain key terms in this series.

GENERAL TERMS

Improvisation

'Improvisation' is the basis of most Drama work. It implies the creation of something new from other resources. Making a still image or soundscape involves improvising, as does re-enacting a story or incident. Hot-seating someone is improvising, as is someone speaking out as if they were in a formal meeting.

Students need some freedom in the way they use a stimulus as the basis of an improvisation if their own creativity and technical skills are to develop. However, teachers also recognise that it is through their improvisations that students reveal the existing limits of their dramatic ability. The task then is to guide the students into new areas of experience and to facilitate activity which will help them develop their skills and knowledge.

Acting

Acting involves some kind of pretence: someone imitates someone other than himself or herself, or perhaps keeps his or her own character, but pretends to be in a different time or place. Within the term 'acting', two other terms are used – 'characterisation' and 'role play' – which are worth distinguishing.

Sometimes, *creating a character* with an apparently realistic psychology and background can stimulate questions about a situation and provide new insights for both the actor playing the character and those who are responding to the playing. For example, a student may adopt the character of an evacuee who has run away from a foster family. The student imagines what answers the evacuee would give and gives them in a convincing way, so the whole class may come to empathise with the character and understand the pressures on this particular evacuee.

At other times, *playing a role* is more important for the drama. In this case, it is not the personal characteristics of the character that are important but that character's function within a given situation. For example, a student might adopt the role of a press reporter assigned to find out about the effect that evacuation has had on a rural community. In this case, playing the reporter 'convincingly' isn't as pertinent as asking the appropriate questions.

A good actor is someone who communicates effectively in a fictitious context. Drama teachers will nurture those elements of the actor's art which allow students to do likewise. In our view, it is perfectly possible to help students develop these skills without denigrating their own personalities and creativity and without relapsing into outmoded and intimidating practices of elocution and deportment!

Teacher-in-Role

By adopting a role within the drama, some teachers find they can break down many of the inhibitions students feel as a result of their consciousness of being watched by a teacher. Like the roles of characters described above, a teacher may adopt a role in order to help the class find something out.

Unfortunately, the technique has acquired a mystique for some teachers who view it with trepidation. The technique is a tool which, like any other, is best used by people who feel comfortable using it, when they think it necessary. It is, however, a particularly effective way of eliciting deep responses from students.

Whole Group Drama

In some ways the term 'whole group drama' seems to be a self-evident objective for any lesson – if the work does not involve the whole group in some way, then it must be less than completely successful! The term has, however, acquired a more specific meaning for many teachers, implying those moments when all the students in the class are actively engaged in an activity in an agreed role. Sometimes this will involve all students acting out a situation spontaneously. For example, they may adopt the role of evacuees while the class teacher, in role as a billeting officer, asks them questions about where they've come from and what the journey was like.

On other occasions, only a small group may be acting while the rest of the class watch with a vested interest. For example, the whole class assume the role of dwellers in a South African township; students watch as a small group improvises a scene in which one member is asked by the authorities to give the names of all those in the township who have been involved in recent protests.

Working as a whole group can be extremely satisfying but shouldn't become a labour. When staying in role begins to feel slavish or unacceptably unruly, our reaction would be to stop the work, discuss what has gone wrong and find a new way forward.

PARTICULAR STRATEGIES

These notes outline the specific strategies used to explore the resources in the Students' Books. This is certainly not a definitive list and many Drama specialists will be able to add other variations or adapt these to their work throughout the school.

Design
Sketching costumes or sets can help build a dramatic context; it introduces the idea that meanings are imparted through the visual aspects of dramatic art. For example:
- The class, in role as police artists, sketch the interior of the coaching inn where a murder appears to have taken place. The exact contents of the room may give important clues and must be detailed.

Forum Theatre
This is a particularly useful way of focusing and developing arguments. Both those involved in a meeting and those observing might call a halt in order to discuss other strategies which the players might take. This technique is explained further in context.

Games
Games in themselves are not Drama, although they can highlight elements of it. For example:
- The class play 'What's the time, Mr Wolf?' and discuss the idea of tension and climax. This is then used in a scene depicting a public execution. Another group plays 'I Spy', as if eighteenth century travellers, in order to build a context for the characters.

Hot-Seating
A character from the drama sits on the 'hot-seat' and is asked questions about himself or herself or about a situation that has arisen in the drama. The questioners may be in a particular role or may just be themselves. For example:
- The students, as themselves, ask someone who was evacuated (perhaps the teacher in role) what he or she remembers most clearly about the War.

Imaging
Imaging is a variation of tableau. Students create a visual image which reflects some elements of the work in hand. This may not involve human characters at all. The students might decide that to make sense the image demands some movement or sound. For us, the concept of making an image through the use of sound, space, movement and gesture is at the heart of dramatic art. For example:
- After reading a poem which describes a police raid on a township in South Africa, the students create an image reflecting what they perceive to be the underlying feelings – pain, hatred, fear, brutality. The image uses space and abstract shapes to express the emotions caught in the poem. A series of words relating to South Africa and Apartheid are spoken by the performers.

Interview

An interview is a more intimate way of extracting or developing the same sort of information gained through hot-seating. Students work in pairs or small groups, and all of them will be in role. For example,

• A hostile TV reporter presses an anti-Apartheid demonstrator about her protest.

Meeting

Meetings generally involve the whole class, who may or may not have a corporate aim. For example:

• A group of teachers reviews the unsatisfactory conditions presented to its evacuee charges. Spokespeople from the South African authorities meet people from a township who have complained about harassment.

Mime

Mime is a highly specialised form of acting. It is a popular activity in many Drama lessons, but fostering mime skills for their own sake may not be very relevant to the needs of most children at Key Stage 3. In these books, we use mime in conjunction with other tasks. For example:

• A group, in role as South African school children, depicts the events of an enforced eviction.

Movement

Movement involves communicating an idea or atmosphere physically. This doesn't necessarily mean using the conventions commonly associated with mime or dance. For example:

• A group depicts travelling through a time warp from the eighteenth century to the present day. The students try to capture both the movement of the journey and its strangeness for the travellers.

Narration

Younger students often narrate their acting unnecessarily or clumsily. However, narration can be linked to theatrical conventions such as the Greek Chorus or the aside, and can give effective insights into a character or situation. For example:

• A small group shows a series of still pictures marking memorable incidents on a stage-coach journey. The pictures are introduced by a narrator who is reading from his or her diary of that journey.

Presentation

Presenting material not originally intended for dramatic presentation can highlight what the elements of Drama are. For example:

• Having read a poem about how beautiful but despised South Africa is, some students present it in a rehearsed reading, using their voices, the space and physical movement to help communicate its meanings.

Sometimes the presentation may be of a piece of script or an improvisation that has been prepared.

Role-on-the-Wall

Characters can be created by drawing a large outline of a figure on a sheet of paper or card. Students fill up the inside of the figure with ideas about the character's physical features, personal details and character traits. Sometimes it is useful to add, outside the outline, ideas about what other people feel and think about the character in order to introduce the notion of perspective.

- Pupils jot down their ideas about an important local figure. They take it in turns to use these notes to show how this character moves and speaks. The pupils brainstorm ideas regarding how the character is perceived by different members of the public. Again, they improvise the reaction of people when the character enters or speaks to them, etc.

Showing Work

Groups can be very insistent that they show their work. This can be time-consuming and tedious. If the group has been given a clear instruction to find something out through its work, then simply reporting back may be more productive. When work is shown, a showing gains dynamic purpose if the audience are given a specific task such as considering how a particular character reacts to the situation. The audience's comments may be used to develop the work by suggesting alternative strategies that the character may have taken; the presentation becomes a part of the process rather than an end product.

Small Group Work

Asking the class to divide into small groups to tackle a task is a common strategy in the Drama lesson. Good work usually depends on good support and advice from the teacher.

Soundtracking

Selecting and taping appropriate music or sound effects to accompany a piece of drama demands careful evaluation and technical expertise. Soundtracking might physically create sounds and rhythms to capture atmosphere or location. For example:

- A traveller in the days of highwaymen must pass through a notorious tract of forest. Every sound seems amplified and threatening. The students create a soundscape of the forest, using their voices and bodies.

Tableau

A tableau is sometimes called a freeze frame or a still image. Students recreate the positions of characters in a particular situation. Tableau is a productive way of slowing down the action and focusing on what is happening to the characters in the drama. For example:

- A group stands as if in a photograph of evacuees waiting for the train to take them away from home. The rest of the class discuss what the positions adopted by those children in the photograph reveal about their attitudes and characters.

Telegram

The language of a telegram is precise and minimal. In Drama, the telegram form can be developed into captions for still images, summarising arguments or describing scenes. The skill of producing a well-chosen line pertains to all forms of literary art. For example:

- Two spies meeting in a crowded inn test each other's identity and exchange messages as quickly and inconspicuously as possible.

Thought-Tracking

In the same way as a cartoon 'thinks bubble' shows a reader something which isn't clear visually, 'thought-tracking' invites students to say aloud what their character might be thinking at a particular moment.

CLASSROOM STRATEGIES

Some of the strategies listed above require the use of a good space; many of them do not. Drama teachers used to working in a specialist environment may sometimes forget that their classroom-based colleagues use a number of techniques which are also stimulating and worthwhile. Some of these are outlined here:

Audio/Visual Recording

If the equipment, time and space are available, recording the students' work can aid evaluation and introduce skills of selection and perspective.

Creative Writing

We use this term as a 'catch-all' phrase. The value of encouraging students to write poems, plays, stories, fictional letters or newspaper reports is self-evident. When this writing occurs in the context of related practical Drama work, the students' motivation is often markedly increased and the results are generally improved.

Discussion

A well-ordered class discussion on the work in progress or on what the class wish to do next will again aid evaluation of Drama specific work, and allow the students to develop the ability to express their own personal thoughts clearly and value those of others.

Display

Displaying design work, or extracts from journals or scripts, will give the students a sense of the worth of that work and attract interest from other groups who use the space.

Prediction

Reviewing existing data in order to hypothesise what will come next is a skill developed in the study of literature and is equally applicable to Drama.

Reportage

Creating newspaper headlines and stories is a common enough activity in the English classroom. Drama can create a stimulating context for the development of this style of writing. Bringing another class into a Drama session and asking students to report on the events being depicted can provide interesting new insights.

Research

Students' own research should never be undervalued. Any opportunity to set a research task should be taken. What is discovered will feed into and enrich the drama and give a sense of ownership. Research needs to be purposeful. Demanding that students produce their own research projects just to keep them quiet/busy/out of the way is likely to result in disaffection rather than motivation.

STRATEGIES FOR ASSESSMENT

Assessment is a two-way process. A student's reflections on the work will help the teacher evaluate that student's development and serve as a check on the interest-value of the work and the teacher's presentation of it. In addition, the teacher's comments on different elements of the work will give the student a clear idea of its worth and relevance. In any case, assessment should be considered, honest and purposeful; it should never be seen as an odious activity, set just for the sake of it.

Some teachers have devised detailed self-assessment profiles which students complete at the end of half-termly or termly units. In our experience, filling in such profiles has not proved popular, and the comments have not been particularly useful. We have found that evaluative work produced in the context of the drama is more interesting and more informative.

The following notes outline some of the ways in which students can reflect on their own work without losing the impetus of the work.

Critical Commentary

When students show their work in Drama, it is useful to encourage them to be critical. All too often, criticism is far from productive and may have little relevance to what the performers were trying to do. Comments like, 'She went through the door without turning the handle' or, 'He had his back towards us all the time' might be true, but need to be balanced against the purpose and content of the presentation.

A way of focusing the criticisms would be to agree appropriate criteria by which to appraise a presentation before seeing it. Write the criteria down so that they may be referred to in subsequent discussion. For example:
• A group has devised a scene in which an economical wartime recipe is explained. The class decide that more important than the characterisation of the presenter is whether or not the ingredients and process are clearly presented.

Discussion

Simply talking briefly about an activity or resource will fulfil a number of the criteria set out in the Attainment Targets for Speaking and Listening as well as indicating some important basic elements in Drama (awareness of tone, volume, gesture). The students' understanding of the subject or theme in hand will also be apparent in a well-guided discussion.

Evidencing

The teacher stops the work at a key point and asks the students to jot something down on paper which will reflect their feelings at that moment. For example:
• 'Note down, as quickly as you can, exactly how you feel when you realise that you are the last evacuee left on the cart.'
• 'Jot down what your personal reaction is to the scene you have just witnessed between those two characters.'

This 'stop and write' technique may be broadened to include other forms of creative writing. The resultant work can be displayed or kept in personal folders and used to inform later elements of the work.

Journal

Asking a class to keep a journal which records the practical work in a personal way may help students evaluate what they have done and formulate their own ideas on what would be useful and/or interesting to do next. Journals can become tedious diaries kept just for the sake of having something in writing to mark; it is better if the journal is more directly related to the fiction of the drama and reflects the student's creative ability. For example:

• The driver of an eighteenth century stage-coach jots down his perspective on the various adventures his passengers appear to be having.

Working Notebooks

Unlike journals, working notebooks record the actual activities undertaken and the students' perceptions of their development in them. They can help students to identify weaknesses which need rectifying. A danger is that the notebook will be full of things that the students think the teacher wants to hear, rather than an honest self-appraisal.

FURTHER READING

We have found the following books particularly helpful in giving both a theoretical grounding for our work and a wealth of practical ideas.

Drama in Schools   The Arts Council (1992)
Towards a Theory of Drama in Education   Gavin Bolton (Longman, 1979)
New Perspectives On Classroom Drama   Gavin Bolton (Simon & Schuster, 1992)
Time for Drama   Roma Burgess & Pamela Gaudry (Open University Press, 1985)
Drama in the English Classroom   Ken Byron (Methuen, 1986)
Education and Dramatic Art   David Hornbrook (Blackwell, 1989)
Education in Drama   David Hornbrook (Falmer Press, 1991)
GCSE Drama Coursebook   Andy Kempe (Blackwells, 1990)
Teaching Drama   Norah Morgan & Juliana Saxton (Hutchinson, 1987)
Making Sense of Drama   Jonothan Neelands (Heinemann, 1984)
Structuring Drama   Jonothan Neelands (Cambridge University Press, 1990)
Drama Structures   Cecily O'Neill & Alan Lambert (Hutchinson, 1982)
Drama Strategies   Ken Taylor (Heinemann, 1991)
The Arts 5–16: A Curriculum Framework   NFAE (Oliver & Boyd, 1990)

CHAPTER 5

EVACUEES *– whole chapter*

INTRODUCTION

The materials in this chapter deal with many of the things that students in the 10–13 age group are concerned with: independence, friendship, loyalties, the attitudes of adults and peers. These issues are tackled by focusing on four stories, based on actual accounts, about the evacuation of people in World War Two.

Kim: An Evacuee's Tale

This offers the students a chance to empathise with someone of their own age who must now face up to a new life without the support she is used to. The material helps students to review their own knowledge and understanding of their place in the social structure by asking:
– To what extent do young people feel powerless in a world dominated by adults?
– What hopes and fears do young people have when faced with change?
– How able are young people at managing on their own?

Mrs Peacock: A Teacher's Tale

This invites the students to review the responsibility involved in looking after others. The supporting material asks the students to consider:
– Why were some children 'more acceptable' than others?
– What sort of problems arise when strangers are injected into a society?
– How do people with responsibility for others manage their situation?

Lesley: A Host's Tale

This tackles young people's egocentricity and raises questions about the relationship between individuals and society:
– How can people share what they see as theirs with someone else?
– How can people with different cultural backgrounds become successfully integrated? Should they be asked to integrate at all?
– What sacrifices are people prepared to make for the 'good of all'?

Martin: A Refugee's Tale

This opens out the topic of evacuation to include all those people who have left their homes to find safety or have been forced to leave because they were not wanted. The key questions in this unit underlie all the resources and touch on many others:
– Why do people sometimes have to leave their homes?
– Who decides who is to move and where they are to go?
– What is the effect of such an experience on the individual?

S t r u c t u r e s

Much of the material (both documentary and fictitious) produced on the evacuees of World War Two focuses on those children who were taken from inner cities to the countryside. Many heartwrenching stories arose around such children, often as a result of the vastly different lifestyles. However, to concentrate on the experiences of this one group at the expense of other stories can lead to cliché and even romanticism, which makes it difficult for students engaged in exploring the material to see the relevance of the subject to their own lives.

The three structures below offer frameworks in which the resource material on evacuees can be used to raise questions pertinent to the lives of today's students.

A Hidden Histories
The students investigate a derelict school once used in the evacuation. They use what they discover as the basis for a 'living museum', the worth of which is challenged by a local councillor.

B Far From Home
The students adopt the role of evacuees and experience a number of incidents from this new perspective.

C Pulling Together
The students adopt the role of trainee evacuation officers. They consider a number of 'case studies' and are then faced with a real situation.

STRUCTURE A: HIDDEN HISTORIES

Aims:

- To encourage the students to look at popular history.
- To stimulate active research and an interest in students' own community.
- To assess the value of local culture.

1 Use the photograph of the old schoolroom (Students' Book, p.38) to stimulate discussion on that period of the War. Students note the differences between then and now by *reading the images* in the photograph.

2 The class imagine that the photograph was taken in a local school which is now to be pulled down. Using *teacher-in-role* as the school caretaker, the students are asked if they will help clear out some old cupboards before the demolition men move in. They are invited to speculate on what they might find of any value.

3 In a period of *hot-seating*, the school caretaker answers questions from the students about what the old school used to be like during the War.

4 The class *mime* exploring the derelict school while *narration* is used to help build a mental picture of it. For example:

- *Look at these old desks. How are they different from the ones you use?*
- *What about those lights? Can you describe them?*

5 The students *mime* clearing the building of desks, cupboards, boxes, etc., while you, in role as the caretaker, check what they are moving and continue to build the context. Some students find interesting items during this exercise and are asked to put them to one side until they can share them with the whole class.

6 Students describe and discuss what they have found. If one of the finds is dubious ('We've found an unexploded bomb!'), the class as a whole can decide whether or not they are prepared to accept it – this can help to rule out some of the more dubious items. A list is made of the finds.

7 Various options will become possible here.
- The caretaker is invited back to talk about the items found.
- Direct reference is made to the Students' Book for information and activities focusing on some of the finds (gas masks, ration books, etc.).
- Other characters who might furnish the class with information are hot-seated.
- Mrs Peacock's Tale is used as a find. What aspects of the evacuation does this make the students want to research further?
- Small groups show how and why the found object came to be in the school.

8 The class look at the 'School Log Book' (Students' Book, p.63) and attention is drawn to the line regarding the last evacuee going home.
- What does this tell the class about the school?
- What might it suggest about that evacuee (parents dead, or displaced, home bombed, etc.)?

9 The class refer to 'Some Background' (Students' Book, pp. 9–10) and discuss any surprises there. A number of routes forward are possible:
- How was the evacuation organised? What was it like? Follow through sections on 'The Call To Go' (Students' Book pp. 14–17) and 'The Journey' (Students' Book, pp. 17–21).
- What was the effect of the evacuees on the receiving areas? Follow through 'Lesley: A Host's Tale' (Students' Book, pp. 40–44) and 'Different Worlds' (Students' Book, pp. 44–6).
- What was school life like for the evacuees? Follow through the sections on 'School Life' (Students' Book, pp. 37–9) and 'Air-Raids and Shelters' (Students' Book, pp. 51–5).
- The class provide other pages from the school log book. These are treated as 'finds' and used to stimulate students' original work.

10 The students make a *living museum* of the old school's history. It might include:
- audio- or video-recorded stories of the school's history;
- displays of written or visual material about the school in the evacuation.

11 The students may wish to work towards presenting this work to other classes or to the rest of the school. They discuss the appropriate format and sequence.

12 In role as a local council official who has heard about the research/museum project, you object to the museum on the grounds that it is dragging up memories best forgotten. (Here you are working as Devil's advocate, trying to get the students to explain and defend their work.)

13 The 'councillor' sets a challenge: either the class find a way of convincing him or her that popular local history, such as the school's, is worth investigating, or the councillor will have the exhibition removed to make way for a display about the council's new civic scheme.

Refer to the 'Going Home' section (Students' Book, pp. 61–4) as a means of generating material which may 'convince' the councillor on his or her next visit.

From here, the length and depth of the drama must be negotiated with the class. One way of appraising the resultant work would be to invite the councillor figure back. Does it satisfy him or her? Will the councillor support the museum project? How well does the exhibition convince the councillor that local culture has a value?

STRUCTURE B: FAR FROM HOME

Aims:

- To develop students' commitment to dramatic roles.
- To explore the themes of loneliness and peer group pressure.
- To encourage students to make a sensitive personal response to stimuli through the dramatic form.

1 The class discuss what images are conjured up by the word 'evacuees' and record ideas of the feelings which might be involved in being evacuated.

2 Students read the narrative of 'Kim: An Evacuee's Tale' and discuss the questions following it (Students' Book, pp. 6–8).

3 Students *read the images* of the two pictures of evacuees waiting for transport (pp. 15 and 16) and work through the tasks.

4 The class decide which group they would be most interested in investigating as evacuees. Consider a situation in which the chosen group would find conflict: the middle-class group might find itself in an impoverished rural community; the less well-off group is faced with a particularly wealthy host community.

5 The students *narrate* the story of the evacuation morning from their chosen perspective.

6 Students fill in a luggage label with a name and address to match their chosen group and tackle task **3** from 'The Call To Go' (Students' Book, p.14) to develop a scene about leaving home.

7 Using task **2** from 'The Call To Go' (Students' Book, p.14), the students develop a piece of drama on what the evacuees might have taken with them.

8 The students use *dramatic play* and *tableaux* to explore what the journey might have been like (see tasks **1** and **2** of 'The Journey' (Students' Book, p.20). Working alone, they write letters from an evacuee's parent or carer.

9 The class explore how the evacuees will be received by using the section on 'Preparing the Hosts' (Students' Book, pp. 25–7). The tasks here are considered in terms appropriate to the characters the class have chosen. For example, the worries of the local people and the advice of a billeting officer will depend on whether this is a poor area expecting wealthy evacuees or a wealthy area expecting urchins. The drama will emerge from a situation offering cultural conflict.

10 The students enact the scene in which the evacuees arrive in the new town/ village. The billeting officer (*teacher-in-role*) introduces them to the place, using details created in the previous exercise. *Thought-tracking* is used to reveal the evacuees' first impressions of their new home. Small groups *improvise* the scene that follows.

11 OPTION ONE

Older or more experienced students may work on their own and choose tasks from the sections on 'Finding Homes' (Students' Book, pp. 28–31), 'Settling In' (pp. 31–4), 'Problems' (pp. 34–7) and 'Different Worlds' (pp. 44–6). They are reminded that the aim is to try to understand the sort of culture shock their chosen characters might experience.

Student journals will help the teacher monitor each group's progress.

12 OPTION TWO

You may wish to keep the class working together to investigate the following ideas.

(*a*) What sort of homes would be strangest to the evacuees? The students look at the pictures of the stately home (p.29) and the farmworker's hovel (p.36), and then follow tasks **1–4** of 'Finding Homes' (Students' Book, pp. 29–31).

(*b*) What memories would the evacuees have of where they were evacuated to? Use tasks **1** and **2** of the section on 'Problems' (Students' Book, pp. 36–7).

(*c*) What would the evacuees' new school be like? Use task **1** from the section on 'School Life' (Students' Book, p.39).

(*d*) What happened when an evacuee ran away? Adopt the role of the headmaster and demand to know where one evacuee has gone. Students answer questions in role and re-enact the last time they were with the runaway. The scenes are reviewed in order to see if they indicate any reasons why the child may have gone. (Various characters are interviewed/hot-seated in order to find out more about the runaway's experience.)

A search of the runaway's possessions reveals helpful evidence (letters, postcards, diary, etc.) which the class create to illustrate why the child ran away. The class decide what actually happened to the runaway, given the wartime situation.

13 The students imagine that, 50 years on, they have been asked to contribute to a programme about the evacuees in a series called *The Happiest Years of Our Lives*. What personal stories would they tell or want enacted for such a progamme? Students construct the programme and possibly share the work with an invited audience, using the section on 'Going Home' (Students' Book, pp. 61–4) to help structure their work.

14 At the end of the programme, the class reflect, in role as the ex-evacuees, on what they think they learned from their experience.

STRUCTURE C: PULLING TOGETHER

Aims:

- To examine the concept of responsibility.
- To challenge assumptions about responsibility through role playing a confrontational situation.
- To stimulate research of a contemporary situation and encourage the students to develop that research into their own drama.

1 Tell the students that over the next few lessons they will be working in role as men and women training to take responsibility for people who have been resettled in an emergency.

2 The room is rearranged to represent a government building. On a board is written: EVACUATION OFFICER TRAINING COURSE.

In role as the training course leader, explain that course members are volunteers who will be trained through a number of specially prepared tasks and role plays. (The resettlement of a large number of people is becoming an increasing possibility, owing to the worsening situation.)

3 The class list people who have, for some reason, been forcibly moved from their homes. The class decide what the 'worsening situation' is, i.e. who *may* need to be evacuated and why.

There is no need at this point to get too involved in details. The purpose of the discussion is simply to give a sense of reality to the Drama work that follows.

4 Tell the students that the first case study concerns the mass evacuation of children in World War Two. Use the tasks from the Introduction to set the context (Students' Book, p.4).

5 Students read 'Kim: An Evacuee's Tale' (Students' Book, pp. 6–8) and 'Some Background' (Students' Book, pp. 9–10). In role as trainee officers, they discuss:
   - What responsibilities are implied for evacuation officers (what they would have done had they been there).
   - From what they have read, what sort of problems they suppose those responsible for the evacuation had.

Small groups depict an incident from 'Kim: An Evacuee's Tale' which they think a trained evacuation officer could have dealt with well. The incident is dramatised and discussed with the rest of the group.

6 The students read the letter reprinted in 'The Call To Go' (Students' Book, p.14). They discuss how appropriate the language would be today and rewrite it for a contemporary situation.

7 Using the information and tasks set in 'Gas Masks' (Students' Book, pp. 11–13), students work out strategies which they think would ensure that children were looked after and could use their masks.

8 The students explore how they, as billeting officers, would find homes for the evacuees. (Use 'Preparing the Hosts', tasks **1–2** (Students' Book, p.27).) The students then look at the photograph of children on the doorstep in 'Finding Homes' (Students' Book, p.28), and the extract from *The Dolphin Crossing* (Students' Book, p.30), and tackle tasks 3 and 4.

9 The students imagine a scene in which a billeting officer is trying to place an evacuee with a householder. What does each party want from the situation? What would be a fair compromise?

The class is divided into three groups: group A to represent a billeting officer; group B, a householder; group C, an evacuee. The groups are given a few minutes to consider what they want from the situation. For example:
   - For group A, placing evacuees is a job, and everyone should be willing to help out.
   - Group B already has children and little money; if an evacuee is to be placed, he or she must be willing to work.
   - Group C has promised parents to keep up with schoolwork; good education may eventually help to bring peace!

Each group picks a representative and *forum theatre* is used to explore possible outcomes of the scene. The scene is opened by the billeting officer saying, 'I'm looking for a home for this evacuee . . .'

10 The students, in role as trainee evacuation officers, use the poster of the mother and children in 'The Phoney War Ends' (Students' Book, p.47) and consider what the mother's responsibilities are. Tasks **1–4** are used to explore how propaganda may be employed to influence public thinking.

11 The section on 'Rationing' (Students' Book, pp. 56–61) is studied and the students consider:
   – what responsibilities the ordinary citizen would have in times of rationing;
   – what responsibilities a food manufacturer or clothing industry would have during rationing.

The class is divided into two:

- Group A devises and presents a wartime cookery programme (task **1**).
- Group B devises and presents a wartime advertisement (task **5**).

The whole class *hot-seat* Miss O'Sullivan (task **4**). They discuss what Miss O'Sullivan's responsibilities are and what they think are the responsibilities of those who set her punishment.

12 In role as the course leader, announce that the situation has worsened and that the evacuation officers must now put into practice what they have learned about responsibility and organisation. (Out of role, the students remind themselves who it is that will need to be evacuated and why.) In role as evacuation officers, the students decide where the new evacuees will go and how the operation should be organised. Possible situations could include one of the following:

- An environmental disaster in another country has forced people to flee. Many have been made ill because of the nature of the disaster (cf. Bhopal, Chernobyl). This country has offered to find temporary homes for many thousands until a more permanent solution can be found. The evacuation officers must find people willing to look after some very sick evacuees of all ages.
- A political upheaval has caused thousands of people to seek new homes. This country has offered places, despite the fact that the evacuees' own country has threatened action against anyone who interferes.
- An impending disaster in one part of the country means that the evacuation officers must organise an immediate evacuation. Many of the local people do not wish to leave (cf. Mount St Helen's, San Francisco earthquake, etc.).

Clearly, there is an opportunity for the class to investigate a current news items here. The drama focuses on these questions: *'If you were responsible for resettling these people, what would you see as the main problems? How would you try to tackle them?'*

13 After working through their own drama on an evacuation, the students read 'Martin: A Refugee's Tale' (Students' Book, pp. 65–6). In the light of their work as 'evacuation officers', what are students' feelings about this story? What conclusions have they come to about the nature, causes and effects of evacuation?

Resources

INTRODUCTION (pp. 4–5)

I Brainstorming

Whole class   5 mins

Objective: To gather and share knowledge about World War Two.

Get the students to say what they *think* they know about the War. Some statements may be factually incorrect. Ask the rest of the students if they agree, leave question marks against statements on which they remain undecided and encourage the class to check them later.

2 and 3 Discussion

Groups: 3–6   10 mins

Objectives: To contribute to a small group discussion.
              To use research to inform discussion.

Students share their knowledge and test what they *think* they know; encourage them to research any questions raised.

4 Presentation

Groups: 3–6   15 mins (preparation)

Objective: To use a dramatic form to communicate ideas.

Some groups may produce very stereotyped images, perhaps excessively violent. The following points may be raised:
– Where do these images come from?
– Do they really reflect what it was like?
– Why do some films etc. depict such exciting images?

KIM: AN EVACUEE'S TALE (pp. 6–21)

The Narrative (pp. 6–8)

I Hot-Seating

Whole class   15 mins

Objective: To reflect on content of a written narrative.

Invite the class to sit in a semi-circle around an empty chair. Before meeting 'Kim', students agree on what they already *know* about her from the story. Each student offers one detail:

- She was quite young when the War broke out.
- Her whole school is being evacuated.
- She doesn't live in London.

Go around the semi-circle a second time. This time, informed assumptions are added, for example:

- She is about thirteen years old.
- The school she goes to is in a run-down area.
- She lives in a northern city.

If the students could ask Kim a single question, what would it be?

Sit on the empty chair and invite the students to ask their questions. A group already used to hot-seating might prefer to have a student play Kim.

2 Small Group Work
Groups: 3–5   10 mins
Objective: To develop a dramatic character appropriate to context.

Encourage the students to focus their work by asking themselves:
– 'Does our scene use what we already know about Kim?'
– 'Does our scene add to that knowledge?'

Some Background (pp. 9–11)

I Research
The chart of the War's key events (Students' Book, p.5) will help students make connections between pieces of knowledge they already have. Encourage them to make links with current events in Europe and suggest a wider application of the term 'evacuee'.

2 Evidencing
Individuals   5 mins
Objective: To use factual evidence in a fictitious narrative.

The time-travel element suggested here may need talking through with the students to avoid confusion.

3 Meeting
Whole class/groups   30 mins
Objective: To use a dramatic role to explore a problem.

Adopting the role of the newly-appointed team leader would be an effective way of keeping the meeting focused:

- Outline the recent events in Europe and the purpose of the meeting, stressing the need to work quickly and efficiently.
- Use the points listed in the Students' Book as examples of the sort of decisions to be made.

- Ask for suggestions as to how the class might most effectively be divided in order to tackle the various tasks.

DEVELOPMENT

Different groups are given specific tasks: writing leaflets for parents, teachers and hosts, deciding on the order of evacuation. Pose new questions to groups:

- Should there be a limit on the amount of luggage?
- What provision will be made for the disabled?
- What qualifications should local billeting officers have? How will you test them?

Gas Masks (pp. 11–13)

1 Mime
Individuals   5 mins
Objective: To further language development.

It may seem odd to suggest a mime to develop language but, by taking away the requirement to speak words aloud, students can reflect on which words are most appropriate to the situation. Use the words collected in this way as the basis for creative writing about gas masks.

2 Small Group Work
Groups: 3–5   10 mins
Objective: To focus a piece of drama for a specific audience.

Encourage students to consider the need to use appropriate criteria in the assessment of work. In this case, they must consider the effectiveness of the game for a very specific purpose.

3 Design
Individuals/pairs
Objective: To use visual elements of Drama to communicate an idea.

The concept of propaganda is often an emotive one. Ask students to consider whether they think making this sort of poster is 'fair'. Under what circumstances would it be 'unfair' to give people advice in this way?

4 Small Group Work
Groups: 3–6   10 mins
Objective: To create a dramatic scene using appropriate characterisation.

Allow the students to work at their own level. Some may experiment with flashback or movement, while others may simply present a naturalistic domestic scene. The response will allow you to gauge what new dramatic experiences the class may need to encounter.

The Call To Go (pp. 14–17)

I Tableau (p.14)

Groups: 3–5   10 mins

Objective: To discuss the use of visual elements of Drama.

In reviewing the tableaux, ask the class to suggest what the characters might be thinking. Is it the same as what they might be saying?

2 Mime/Evidencing

Individuals   5 mins

Objective: To relate mime skills to a specific context.

Students describe what they have done and what they felt immediately after the exercise. Written work generated in this way may usefully be shared through display or reading.

3 Small Group Work

Groups: 4–8   10 mins

Objective: To create a dramatic scene appropriate to the stimulus.

I Small Group Work (p.16)

Groups: 4–6   25 mins

Objective: To create dialogue appropriate to a character.

Reflect on the origins of people's perceptions of events and images. For example, all the groups acting out the scene in the photograph on p.16 may choose to talk with 'tally-ho' voices. Why? What is the class's own response to such a depiction? Why? Does the use of accent affect the degree of sympathy we have for the characters?

2 Interview

Pairs   5 mins

Objective: To ask relevant questions and relate imaginary events.

'Spotlight' work by asking the rest of the class to stop and listen to one pair on their own. Comment on the different approaches being taken and the attitudes being exhibited by the characters. Is B sympathetic or looking for sensational details of woe?

3 Reportage

Individuals

Objective: To produce a piece of impersonal writing for a specified audience.

The Journey (pp. 17–21)

I Thought-Tracking/Role Play

Whole class   15 mins

Objective: To describe an imagined scene in role.

Making the train up will require considerable group co-operation. Build commitment to the drama by describing the journey so far.

2 Narration/Tableau
Groups: 3–6   10 mins
Objective: To use visual images to tell a story.

Students tend to be accustomed only to the naturalistic style of TV and need to be encouraged to experiment with other forms which reflect, rather than imitate, real life.

3 and 4 Evidencing
Individuals
Objective: To produce a piece of creative writing in role.

Encourage students to share their writing. An appropriate way to do this would be to use the script as an integral part of a dramatic image such as that created in task **4**.

5 Presentation
Groups: 2–3   10 mins
Objective: To use gesture and movement to show a dramatic relationship.

Encourage students to experiment with communicating meaning through the use of space, movement and gesture.

6 Creative Writing
Individuals

7 Song
Individuals/pairs
Objective: To employ vocal skills in a dramatic context.

Many teachers and students are reluctant to use song. Advertising jingles, playground songs and parodies like the example given are ways of overcoming this reluctance. Try singing them as a round or as a 'bar-room' choir, simply to get everyone joining in and more used to singing.

MRS PEACOCK: A TEACHER'S TALE (pp. 22–39)

The Narrative (pp. 22–3)

1 Research
Pairs   20 mins
Objective: To contribute ideas about the content and form of a piece of drama and to find an appropriate way of recording it.

Some initial guidance with this task may help considerably: work through one example as a whole group, then allow students to develop another in pairs.

2 Presentation
Groups: 3–8   15 mins
Objective: To consider the qualities of a variety of dramatic forms.

Students will be familiar with buildings collapsing on TV and film, but stage presentation demands other strategies. Perspective, timing, reportage and chorus could all be introduced at this level of work.

3 Meeting/Role Play

Whole class   20 mins
Objective: To use a dramatic role to explore a problem.

It may be useful to adopt a low status here, such as the most junior member of the group. From this position, you can support the students' roles by placing them in a position of authority (they have what Dorothy Heathcote would call 'the mantle of the expert'). Asking for clarification of material reviewed so far or reporting an incident which demands immediate attention puts a responsibility on the students to take their role seriously.

4 Creative Writing

Individuals
Objective: To similate the style and content of a piece of prose and develop it
                        appropriately.

Preparing the Hosts (pp. 25–7)

1 Interviews

Pairs   5 mins
Objective: To ask and respond creatively to relevant questions.

Details of work generated here will be useful in the following exercise; ask students to jot down key ideas directly after the exercise.

2 and 3 Document Writing/Meeting

Whole class   20 mins
Objectives: To use an appropriate style of formal writing.
                        To sustain a dramatic character appropriate to the situation.

An alternative to setting individuals a written task would be to adopt the role of a senior official responsible for billeting evacuees in the area. Students play volunteer billeting officers. In a meeting situation, the class discuss the following questions:

- What arguments could be used with households unwilling to accommodate evacuees?
- What are people's responsibilities in the given situation?
- What particular problems might be experienced at a local level?

Draw attention to the memories printed in this section. Clearly, there were many problems. How would this class endeavour to overcome them?

The class could move on to the pamphlet writing task or task **3** without changing roles.

Finding Homes (pp. 28–31)

I Telegram
Groups: 5–7   10 mins
Objective: To use language economically.

The exercise uses the now familiar techniques of tableau and improvisation to generate material which is considered in terms of dramatic effectiveness.

2 Small Group Work
Groups: 2–5   5 mins
Objectives: To describe a fictitious experience in detail.
　　　　　　　To ask relevant questions.

Adopt the role of the owner of the house. Provide the students with some narration, for example:
– the name and a brief history of the house;
– some of its most interesting features (dungeons, priest holes, the family ghost!);
– the importance, as guests, of obeying the house rules.

Having set the tone (you may have chosen to be very austere or perhaps rather eccentric), the class divide into groups which go off with one of the 'servants'.

3 Small Group Work
Groups: 3   15 mins
Objectives: To adapt performance to suit material.
　　　　　　　To employ a variety of dramatic techniques.

Discuss students' own experiences of being in a situation where they were being talked about but did not wholly understand the conversation. The extract presents an interesting dramatic problem: how can you convey something to an audience which a character on stage cannot share?

4 Small Group Work
Groups: 3–5   15 mins
Objective: To use a variety of dramatic forms to communicate a narrative.

5 Creative Writing
Individuals

Settling In (pp. 31–4)

I Design/Telegram
Individuals   10 mins
Objective: To write in role, using language economically.

Using postcards to communicate situations and feelings is a flexible and, because of the limited space available, is an unthreatening means of introducing students to writing in role.

2 Meeting

Whole class   10 mins

Objectives: To use formal language appropriately.

To sustain a dramatic role.

Establish an appropriate 'ritual' for the meeting. Suggest that it would be useful for somebody to chair the meeting, e.g. the headteacher. Depending on the age and experience of the class, invite one of the students to be the headteacher or play the part yourself. If you play the part, ask students to tell you how you should play it. Teachers present in the meeting are asked to report on:

– how well the evacuees took leave of their families;

– whether they managed to bring the right type/amount of luggage with them;

– what problems there were on the journey;

– whether any of the evacuees have any personal problems which will need monitoring.

Reinforce the ritual and formality of the meeting and challenge any inappropriate comments on the grounds of their effect on the scene. If, for example, one of the evacuees is incontinent, how would the teacher convey this in the context of a formal meeting?

3 Creative Writing

Individuals

4 and 5 Imaging

Individuals/small groups   15 mins

Objective: To create a written or dramatic image.

The idea of the last child is a particularly potent one to which many, if not all, students will be able to relate. The fact that it does involve feelings which are so 'close to home' means that there might be some resistance and the task may demand careful and sensitive support.

I Hot-Seating (p.34)

Whole class   15 mins

Objective: To sustain a dramatic character with conviction.

Establish some basic facts about the old man and invite a student to take on the character. Students ask questions about life before and after the arrival of the evacuees.

Decide on four people who may know this old man, for example an evacuee, a teacher, his landlord, etc. Four students adopt these characters in different parts of the room and are quizzed by classmates as to why this old man was so popular with the evacuees. Information gathered from this work is used in small group improvisations that show the relationship between the old man and the evacuees. The scenes must try to use and develop what has already been established about the character.

2 Design (p.34)
Individuals
Objective: To create a visual context appropriate to a dramatic character.

The students assume the role of set designers whose responsibility it is to convey accurately the old man's character through the furnishing and decoration of his room.

3 Small Group Work (p.34)
Groups: 2–6   10 mins
Objective: To develop and sustain a dramatic character.

Assess the work in terms of how well the information generated above has been used and developed.

Problems (pp. 34–7)

1 Small Group Work
Groups: 2–5   5 mins
Objective: To portray dramatic characters appropriate to a situation.

Draw attention to the quotations in this section. What sort of preconceptions and prejudices do they illustrate?

2 Presentation
Groups: 2–5   15 mins
Objective: To explore a conflict through Drama, adapting performance to suit the material.

Share the scenes and ask the class audience to consider the following questions:

- What was the conflict?
- Did the scene show how the conflict arose?
- Did the scene show why people reacted to the conflict as they did?

School Life (pp. 37–9)

1 Meeting
Whole class   10 mins
Objectives: To organise a dramatic space.
To sustain a dramatic role.

Discuss the details of what the classroom should look like, as a whole group, and physically rearrange the furniture accordingly.

Students arrange a tableau which captures the appropriate atmosphere of the 1939 classroom. This is used as the starting point for an improvisation.

DEVELOPMENT

2 Small Group Work

Groups: 3–5   10 mins

Objective: To portray dramatic characters with conviction.

Scenes developed here could stand on their own or be woven into the drama introduced above.

3 Forum Theatre

Whole class   10 mins

Objective: To adopt dramatic roles to explore different perspectives on a given issue.

The class decide what happened to the runaway evacuee. An official complaint is made about the way the Headmaster handled the situation. Divide the class into three large groups:

- Group A will represent the Headmaster. He wishes to impress the Board of Enquiry that his action was justified and necessary.
- Group B will represent the complainant (perhaps a teacher, a parent, a host). He or she wishes to impress upon the Board of Enquiry why the Headmaster's action was wrong.
- Group C will represent the official handling the enquiry. His or her task is to hear both sides of the story.

Representatives of each group seat themselves as if in the office of the official. The meeting is improvised, but at any point the players may stop the improvisation and turn to their 'team' for advice on what to say or do next. Alternatively, a player may be replaced by another member of the team who carries on the argument without changing the role.

4 Telegram

Individuals/pairs   10 mins

Objectives: To use language formally and economically.
To portray dramatic characters with conviction.

LESLEY: A HOST'S TALE (pp. 40–64)

The Narrative (pp. 40–43)

1 Character Study

Individuals

Objective: To record dramatic ideas appropriately.

As well as developing an ability to write economically, the exercise will also reflect the students' developing understanding of dramatic character.

DEVELOPMENT

Encourage students to sketch ideas for costumes, facial attitudes, etc., along with suggestions for characterising gestures, tones of voice, speech patterns, etc.

2 Interview

Pairs   5 mins

Objective: To sustain a dramatic character appropriate to the stimulus.

Use this short exercise to assess the extent to which students have assimilated the narrative.

3 Movement

Groups: 2–5   20 mins

Objectives: To show a practical understanding of the use of space and timing.
To employ movement skills to portray a character.

Encourage students to move away from naturalistic mime and to experiment with creating images which may capture ideas and emotions more directly.

4 Creative Writing

Individuals

5 Small Group Work

Groups: 2–6   15 mins

Objective: To use a variety of dramatic forms to communicate a narrative.

Students will be familiar with the idea of the flashback through film and TV. Make the point that the technique may be used equally well in live theatre.

DEVELOPMENT

Finding an alternative to the classic 'wobbly screen' device for signifying a time shift might well involve introducing simple lighting techniques, for example changing the colour, angle and quality of light.

Different Worlds (pp. 44–6)

1 Interview

Pairs   15 mins

Objectives: To record a dramatic idea.
To adapt performance to suit material.

Guide students on how to phrase scene outlines in a way that offers a starting point but does not predetermine the outcome. For example, compare these two scene outlines:

- A local farm-hand has teased and wasted the time of some evacuees who have kindly offered to help.
- A farm-hand tells some evacuees to go and pick some carrots off the carrot tree. When they learn that carrots don't grow on trees, they get their own back on the farm-hand by pushing him into the dung heap.

Which scene is more likely to produce the most interesting response?   *43*

DEVELOPMENT

In discussing the scenes, students may be guided to comment on how their own ideas translated into dramatic characters. To what extent did the way the characters were portrayed match the perceptions of the originators of the ideas?

2 Scriptwriting
Individuals/pairs
Objectives: To demonstrate some technical knowledge in the recording of a dramatic idea.
To show some understanding of how Drama relates to other arts.

Any of the resource material in the Students' Book may be used as a stimulus for this task. Allow students to browse through the book, scanning for a likely starting point. The exercise provides an opportunity for students to work on their own for some time. The task may be set as an on-going one for students to undertake in their own time, while other activities are covered in class time.

3 Meeting
Whole class   10 mins
Objective: To discuss a dramatic presentation in a cultural and historical context.

Any piece of writing prepared for a specified audience should be assessed accordingly. Considering the effect of material on an audience in this way will help students focus their own work.

DEVELOPMENT

4 Discussion
Whole class
Objective: To discuss and debate constructively.

The role play above may lead to a more general discussion of how 'types' of people are depicted in the media or how different accents or geographical regions are associated with certain types of character. Such work should aim to encourage an awareness of the uses and abuses of stereotyping.

'Stereotyping' is a slippery concept with which Drama teachers frequently struggle. Our view is that using stereotypes in a dramatic depiction is not bad *per se*, and it could be argued that any dramatic characterisation draws on stereotyping to some degree. However, we would encourage students to recognise that some stereotypes are wholly negative and can obscure the purpose of a dramatic presentation.

The Phoney War Ends (pp. 46–51)

1 Design
Individuals
Objective: To focus on and use an appropriate visual style.

Making posters presents the students with the task of communicating the essence of a subject in a direct and stylised way. It encourages awareness of the power of visual imagery, especially when used in conjunction with words.

DEVELOPMENT

Research and discuss other posters of the era and compare their style with that of any current Public Information posters which seem successful.

2 Presentation

Groups: 4–6   20 mins

Objective: To use an appropriate dramatic form to communicate an idea.

Students' Drama work often seems meandering and unfocused. This exercise demands that students have a very clear focus on content and audience. Once the students have shared their scenes, discuss with them what they have learned here about focus.

DEVELOPMENT

A discussion of propaganda will draw attention to the relationship between dramatic style and historical context. To what extent may Government film makers *justifiably* make a situation look worse than it actually is? Do they have the right to frighten people deliberately? Do they have the right to try and make people do what *they* think is best?

3 Storyboard

Groups: 4–6   20 mins

Objective: To record dramatic ideas.

Storyboarding is an extremely useful device which helps students to see their work objectively and to make decisions about style, focus and framing.

4 Interview

Pairs   5 mins

Objective: To ask and respond to questions appropriate to a dramatic role.

5 Meeting

Whole class   15 mins

Objective: Organise a space and sustain a dramatic character.

Options for a teacher's role would include:

- An austere Government official. (The students in role may respond by expressing their frustration with the organisation of the evacuation operation.)
- A local spokesperson who, with help from the class, explains to a student in role as the official, what the feelings about the situation are. The meeting focuses on how to proceed, given those feelings.

In either case, the purpose of the drama is to focus on an issue and explore how the characters deal with it.

DEVELOPMENT

Small groups improvise what happens next, or individuals note their reactions and thoughts through some form of evidencing.

I Movement (p.50)

Whole class   30 mins

Objectives: To employ vocal and movement skills.
To demonstrate an understanding of the importance of space and timing.

Students compare the relative effects of, for example:
– steady, controlled movements/jerky, spasmodic movements;
– large, slow movements/small, fast movements.

Students develop a soundtrack using voices and percussion to fit the movements agreed upon.

2 Thought-Tracking/Creative Writing (p. 50)

Whole class   5 mins +

Objective: To use words appropriate to an imagined situation.

The students stand at one end of the room and imagine that they are looking at the bombed school. Ask individuals to voice details of what they can see. Ask them to jot down their thoughts immediately and develop them later through creative writing.

3 Mime/Movement (p.50)

Groups: 3–6   5 mins

Objective: To use movement skills to create a dramatic atmosphere.

The students must move with precision and find appropriate ways of communicating with each other and working together without words.

Air-Raids and Shelters (pp. 51–5)

I Journal

Individuals   10 mins

Objective: To create a personal piece of writing and develop it for dramatic presentation.

The expressions of the children in the slit trench seem to suggest a range of reactions to the bombers overhead. Consider the following two possibilities:

• Some of the children are used to air-raids. For others it is a new experience.
• The children come from London. The bombers are heading in that direction.

2 Small Group Work

Groups: 4–6   10 mins

Objective: To use language appropriate to a given audience.

Students play a role within a role, i.e. young teachers pretending to be infant children. The purpose of the exercise needs clarification: what language do you use to get children to do something important? The suggestion that the students become young teachers in the role play should help avoid silliness and overacting when in role as the infants.

3 Design

Individuals

Objectives: To draw a plan to specific requirements.

To consider a technical aspect of Drama.

Having investigated the real dimensions of an Anderson shelter, how could the interior of one be effectively shown on stage?

4 Presentation

Groups: 3–6   20 mins

Objective: To adapt performance to suit material.

Rationing (pp. 56–61)

1 Presentation

Pairs   10 mins

Objective: To use a specific dramatic form to communicate to a given audience.

While not underestimating the seriousness of food shortages during the War, it might be valuable to use these recipes for a bit of fun. The work will nevertheless make a point about living conditions in the War and indicate the degree to which the students are aware of, and can manipulate, a particular style of presentation.

DEVELOPMENT

The same objective holds true for task **2**, while task **3** develops the idea into a piece of creative writing.

4 Hot-Seating

Whole class   5 mins

Objective: To sustain a dramatic character and to ask appropriate questions.

In contrast to the light tone of the above presentations, an investigation into Miss O'Sullivan's story highlights a number of issues about austerity, responsibility and compassion. Either adopt her role yourself or invite a student to, and hot-seat the character. Do students have sympathy with Miss O'Sullivan? Is she a lonely old lady or an eccentric, well-off woman who likes birds more than servants? Is the punishment justifiable or does it depend on what Miss O'Sullivan is like?

5 Presentation/Design

Individuals/groups: 3–5   20 mins

Objective: To record or present a dramatic idea in a style which suits the stimulus.

The storyboard advertisements may be developed by different groups to those which originated them.

Going Home (pp. 61–4)

1 Journal

Groups: 2–6   15 mins

Objective: To create a piece of original writing and develop it dramatically.

This may be set simply as a creative writing task but there is the possibility that the most interesting notes in the log book could be 'brought alive' by using flashback, tableaux, soundtracking, etc.

2 Interview

Whole class   30 mins

Objective: To develop interviewing skills such as asking appropriate questions.

Local research among neighbours and relatives can provide a wealth of resources for Drama and writing. Some practice in and reflection on the best techniques in the classroom prior to an actual interview will give the students confidence and help them elicit information more effectively. The following sequence may help prepare them:

- A small number of students act as researchers who are to visit an old people's home.
- The rest of the students will take on the roles of the residents there.
- Before embarking on the improvisation, discuss the questions noted in the Students' Book. Which questions will elicit the most informative answers?
- Improvise the scene in the old people's home in order to try out students' questioning technique. Students playing the residents should feel free to invent personal information in response to the questions.
- After ten minutes, reflect on which questions seemed easiest to answer in detail. What other advice on interviewing technique would the 'residents' give?
- Swap roles, so that all students have an opportunity to test their questioning technique.

Do make sure that appropriate arrangements are made and permission has been granted before instructing students to go out interviewing.

3 Presentation

Whole class   20 mins

Objective: To contribute ideas about content and form appropriate to the context.

The content of the TV programme is clearly important but, perhaps more interestingly, this exercise will help students see the importance of choosing a suitable framing device for Drama.

MARTIN: A REFUGEE'S TALE (pp. 65–8)

This short section opens out the theme of evacuees and raises the issue of why some people are forced to move from their homes.

Firsthand experience, primary source material derived from interviews and current news items may all be used to raise awareness and provide material for dramatic exploration.

The material in the Students' Book on the evacuation in World War Two will give a guide to the resources that can be used to stimulate creative work; the strategies employed in the various tasks are largely transferable.

The section serves as a comparison with other situations. For example, children in the War were evacuated for their own safety, but why were the Boat People evacuated from Hong Kong? Most evacuees were sent to stay with people from the same country and general culture. How does this compare with the experience of, say, a Vietnamese refugee coming to Britain?

A great deal has been written about the evacuees of World War Two, much of it looking back at the period with some sentiment. How much is published about other evacuees? Are their stories told in the same detail or with the same fondness?

Having worked through the material in the Students' Book, individuals or whole classes may wish to embark on a further related study of their own which addresses some of these questions through a range of written forms as well as through practical Drama.

PLAYSCRIPT 'JUST REMEMBER TWO THINGS: IT'S NOT FAIR AND DON'T BE LATE' (pp. 69–76)

This extract from the 1988 radio play by Terence Frisby is included as an endpiece to the Students' Book because it encapsulates many of the feelings and issues tackled in the resources in that book. In his autobiographical tale, Terence Frisby conveys the historical context with humour and sensitivity as he charts the tensions and fun which arose from the differences between town and country life in the War years.

The tasks are divided into four sections:

Acting The Play

These four tasks encourage the students to experiment actively with the practical problems of depicting dramatic characters. Students discuss what emotions and thoughts might lie behind some of the lines, using hot-seating, and begin to see how there is more to playing a dramatic character than just reading the lines on the page.

Task **3** asks the students to experiment with accents. Teachers might be rightly concerned about stereotyping of regional characters here. Despite this, we feel that in the sensitive and controlled environment of the English or Drama room, negative depictions can be challenged while the students are still given the chance to see just what they can do with their voices.

Producing The Play

Some teachers will not have immediate access to a suitable Drama space. These tasks draw special attention to the fact that the extract is taken from a radio play – a form which we believe is of huge potential for young writers as it allows them to create atmospheres without having to rely on sophisticated stage or visual spectacles. As well as writing them, students can often record/perform them more successfully than other forms of Drama.

Task **4** asks the students either to set out physically or imagine the layout of various scenes. If an actual space is not available, the task should still stand as an exercise in design and encourage the students to think about what is really essential in terms of creating a dramatic effect.

Ideas For Drama

These two creative extension tasks ask the students to move beyond the world of the extract and draw upon the resources and work they have encountered in other parts of the Students' Book. Task **1** focuses on the potential of juxtaposing a humorous scene with a serious one. Task **2** subtly pursues this by asking the students to consider the advantages and disadvantages of actually *playing* an emotional scene rather than finding a way of reporting it.

Ideas For Writing

Tasks **1** and **3** give the students a chance to use their writing skills to extend the characters of Terry and Jack. Task **1** could be developed into a piece for reading aloud and perhaps used as the vocal part of a dramatic presentation depicting the scenes on the postcards. Students tackling Task **3** should be encouraged to look back through the Students' Book for ideas about the historical context.

Task **2** focuses on accent and should be seen as a part of work on Knowledge about Language.

FURTHER READING

Novels

Home Before Long	Bill Gillham (André Deutsch, 1983)
Rainbow Cake	Alan Spooner (Kestrel, 1981)
Back Home	Michelle Magorian (Puffin, 1987)
Going Back	Penelope Lively (Heinemann, 1975)
The Dolphin Crossing	Jill Paton Walsh (Macmillan, 1968)
Fireweed	Jill Paton Walsh (Macmillan, 1969)
Goodnight, Mr Tom	Michelle Magorian (Puffin, 1983)
Carrie's War	Nina Bawden (Puffin, 1974)
In Spite of All Terror	Hester Burton (Oxford University Press, 1968)
The Exeter Blitz	David Rees (Hamish Hamilton, 1978)
The Machine Gunners	Robert Westall (Puffin, 1975)
Blitzcat	Robert Westall (Macmillan, 1989)

Plays

Evacuees	Jack Rosenthal (Longman)
Vacuees	Bill Martin (Cambridge University Press)
Just Remember Two Things: It's Not Fair and Don't Be Late	
	Terence Frisby (Methuen, 1986)

Non-fiction

Spotlight on the Second World War	Nathaniel Harris (Wayland Books Ltd)
The Second World War	C. A. R. Hills (Batsford, 1981)
We'll Meet Again	Robert Kee (Dent, 1984)
Bombers and Mash	Raynes Minns (Virago, 1980)
The People's War	Angus Calder (Cape, 1969)
Children of the Blitz	Robert Westall (Penguin, 1985)
No Time to Wave Goodbye	Ben Wicks (Bloomsbury, 1988)

CHAPTER 6: THE GREAT BATH ROAD

INTRODUCTION

We have deliberately made the heroine of this tale very naïve. However naïve and passive, we hope she isn't offensive in herself but a means by which today's young people can explore a range of issues such as:

- crime and punishment;
- disparity of wealth and power;
- popular mythology;
- the destructive nature of stereotypes.

Passive observation of these things isn't an option: through practical Drama work, students are encouraged to explore the implications of these issues and assess their own position on them.

On a different level, we hope the work will generate an interest in:

- local customs, traditions and history;
- Non-Standard forms of English;
- pre-twentieth century literature;
- non-narrative forms of writing.

The inspiration for this work has come from the picaresque novels of the eighteenth century, such as Henry Fielding's *Tom Jones*, Tobias Smollett's *Humphrey Clinker* and Daniel Defoe's *Moll Flanders*. Though they tell a rollicking good story, these episodic novels also offer a sharp critique of eighteenth-century society. Our Heroine is also indebted to Jane Austen's depiction of Catherine Morland in *Northanger Abbey* for her innocence about the real world and contrasting addiction to the gothic romance. Rather sadly perhaps, neither the style of the eighteenth-century novel, nor the period itself, has been particularly well explored in children's literature or drama. For a period as rich in artistic innovation as it was poor in social justice and world vision, it offers a lens through which we might usefully inspect our current society.

Structures

The structures below focus on three aspects of the eighteenth century. Each draws on the historical material in the Students' Book and encourages the students to develop literary and dramatic skills to shape their own response to the contradictions of this fascinating period.

A Journey

With this structure, the students are asked to identify with a group of children in a rural community in the eighteenth century.

As they go on their journey from childhood to adulthood, the rapidly changing face of the country is reflected in the changing use of the road which passes through their village. Ultimately, they are faced with an adult decision to which the road itself offers a possible solution: do they go or do they stay?

B Mapping Out New Stories

With this structure, the students are introduced to the idea of 'mapping' a text. The process facilitates a manipulation and reordering of the events recorded in the Students' Book in order to make a new story from a new perspective. This work will highlight the importance of narrative structure, the way characters are constructed and how different tellings of stories reveal different viewpoints.

C 'An Actor's Life For Me!'

How would an eighteenth-century actor-manager treat Our Heroine's journal on stage? This structure uses both the factual and fictitious material in the Students' Book as the basis for an exploration of the theatre craft of the period. Many of the myths and expectations popularly held today about the theatre stem from this period. While celebrating the exuberance and innovation of the eighteenth-century theatre, this structure places its practices firmly in a cultural and historical context.

STRUCTURE A: JOURNEY

Aims:

- To explore the effect of the road on the lives of the people who lived near it.
- To create a drama in an historical context, with an 'authentic' situation and lifelike characters.
- To investigate the narrative potential of time and space.

1 Using the questions on p.1 of the Introduction, ask the students what sort of journeys they make on a regular basis. Note their responses and then ask them about the best and worst journeys they have ever made.

2 In small groups, the students make *still images* of scenes which show themselves *before* and *after* either a good or bad journey.

3 The group discusses how some journeys change people forever. Each student creates a *tableau* and thinks of a line which a character might think or say which will make it absolutely clear who he or she is and also show the nature of his or her significant journey, for example:

- 'I can't stay here any longer, Mum. I'm going to find a place of my own!'
- 'Have you got the ring in your pocket? Check it now before we go.'
- 'This is boring! Let's get back to the house to hear the reading of the will!'

The lines and tableaux are shared.

4 Ask what other sorts of journeys are sometimes used as the basis for dramas, for example, travel through time and space.

5 Tell students that they are going to start on a drama which will explore the idea of why people make journeys and what the nature of those journeys might be. Explain that the students are on a school coach trip. The students suggest where they are going, and why, and set up chairs to suggest the coach.

6 Commitment to the situation is built up through a soundscape. Against the background noise of the journey, individuals call out lines when you touch them on the shoulder, for example:

- 'Hey, what's that in your lunch box?'
- 'I wonder what we'll miss at school.'
- 'Mr Driver, can we have the radio on, please?'

7 The group uses some songs to build up the coach journey atmosphere. Willy Russell's *Our Day Out* contains some simple and lively ones, for example:

> 'We're off, we're off
> We're off in a motor car
> Sixty coppers are after us
> And they don't know who we are!'

8 In role as the leader of the trip, announce that the coach will pull into a lay-by for lunch. There is a wood there and plenty of places to sit and eat. The class respond through the use of *spontaneous improvisation*.

9 Out of role, narrate how, once off the coach, some of the students notice an old milestone by the lay-by. If at all possible, a small rostrum block should be placed to represent this in the middle of the studio as it will be a focus in the drama to come.

10 Add a particular detail to the narration:

> As you stood by the edge of the road, not knowing which way to go, a strange feeling came over each of you . . . The sort of odd sensation that makes you shiver and say that someone just stepped on your grave . . . For some reason, you flicked your head around to the milestone, and just for an instant this is what you saw . . .

The class look at the photo of the person by the milestone (Students' Book, p.20). Use *thought-tracking* to gather the instant reactions of the students.

11 Out of role, read a passage from Trevelyan's *History of England* to the class:

> Once on this earth, on this familiar spot of ground, walked other men and women, as actual as we are today, thinking their own thoughts, swayed by their own passions, but now all gone, one generation vanishing after another, gone as utterly as ourselves will shortly be gone, like ghosts at cock-crow.

Invite the students to comment on the effect the quotation has on them. The students should then jot down ideas which suggest who the cloaked figure might be and why his or her apparition seems to be linked with the milestone.

12 The students read the extract from *Astercote*, (Students' Book, p.5). In small groups, they work on ways of suggesting, through an *improvised presentation*, that the children who were on the school outing are somehow transported back to a time when a village stood close to the milestone. Given that they can't use devices from TV or the cinema (like the wobbly TV screen), how will they use sound, movement, gesture and perhaps lines of dialogue to suggest travel back in time?

13 In pairs, the students imagine that they are young people who live in the village. It is 1770. One partner guides the other (whose eyes are closed) around the space and points things out to him or her, for example:

– 'In front of you is the church. Tell me what you see as you look at it.'

The unsighted partner adds details:
– 'It's grey and quite small. It has a tower.'

Encourage the sighted partner to elicit more detail, for example:
– 'Is the door open or closed? Tell me about some of the tombs in the churchyard.'

14 Using ideas generated in the improvisation above, the group draws a large map of the village (it may be best if key features such as the road and milestone are already marked, leaving the students to add buildings and other landmarks). While they draw, students narrate details about life in the village:
• Who are the local characters?
• Does anything much ever happen there?
• What sort of interesting people have passed along the road recently?

15 Out of role, use the section explaining why Wiltshiremen are called 'Moonrakers' (Students' Book, p.72) to inform the class that there is an inn in the village which has been named because of a similar local legend. Use tasks **1** and **2** to develop this (Students' Book, pp. 72–3). (This involves asking the students to write an entry in a guide-book and to draw a storyboard. Some might like to draw a large sign to mark the inn.)

16 The class are invited to imagine that the young people who live in the village spend most days helping their parents. Some work in the fields, but the biggest employer in the village is the inn. The resources about inns (Students' Book, pp. 24–6) are read to give an idea of what they were like.

17 The students make a *tableau* showing what the inn yard might look like and think about the job they do there. The tableau is animated, and in a period of dramatic play the class try to capture the atmosphere of the scene. Ask the class to freeze from time to time and use thought-tracking to get an idea of what some of the students are doing. (You may wish to refer to the tasks on 'Coaching Days' – Students' Book, pp. 9–10 – to support this work.)

18 Use *narration* to inform the class that an important visitor is due to arrive today by stage-coach. He is a representative from the Turnpike Trust. (You might use the data in the Students' Book on pp. 39 and 47 to give the class an outline of the work of the Trust, possibly using role-on-the-wall to create a character who might be a Trust member.)

19 The class step back into the *spontaneous improvisation* and at an appropriate moment you enter, in role as the Turnpike Trustee. Emphasise your status by calling on one of the students to relay a message in a loud voice, for example:

> Now, boy, I want you to draw the attention of all of your fellows here to this notice. You can read it out to them – if you can read. Now, I have other business to attend to here, but should any of the people from the village wish to see me, I shall be available in the dining room at noon for a short while.

Hand the student an enlarged copy of the notice on p.40 of the Students' Book.

20 Invite students to react in role to the notice for a few minutes. Freeze the improvisation and briefly interview some members of the group about their reactions. Ascertain what they think this notice might mean to them. You have the chance here to point out that at their age they too would have been required to work on the road. The average wage for adult labourers was about 50p per week – what would a daily fine of 7½p mean to their family?

21 Narrate how someone in the village vandalises the poster with a piece of well-chosen graffiti. Students speculate what the graffiti might have been and write their chosen comment on the poster. Back in role, the students show through improvisation how their characters would react to this unlawful addition.

22 The group decides to meet with the Trustee (teacher-in-role) who gives them further information as to why the road needs more attention (need for improved travel and communications in the rapidly-changing world; the road is a major link between London and Bristol; if it falls into such a bad state of repair, then many merchants may use other routes which would have a bad effect on the village, etc.). The Trustee's arguments are full of threats mixed with promises of riches. You need to play Devil's advocate to encourage a range of responses in the meeting. The drama will be richer if individual characters can clearly be seen as losing or gaining a lot from the situation.

23 If the group decides to undertake the work, use the song on p.38 of the Students' Book with task **1** (p.41) to establish a sense of community among those working on the road. You could follow this up by using tasks **2** and **3** to challenge the students' commitment to their role.

It may be that the group decides to resist the pressure and shows how it gets rid of the Trustee (though it is important that it explores the consequences of its actions).

24 Use the section on local customs (Students' Book, pp. 51–2) to suggest that, despite the impositions of outsiders like the Turnpike Trust, the people in the village had a strong sense of community and a sense of ownership of that part of the road. Although many travellers passed through the village, hardly any of the inhabitants ever went more than a few miles from the village. On a summer's evening, a traveller might see the young people skipping in the dust of the road or playing games for which only they seemed to know the rules. Others might be sitting at the roadside, speculating on what lay at the end of the road in either direction . . .

Ask the class to split into groups and invent a ritual game or a skipping rhyme which might have been played or sung at the time.

25 Use the drama on smuggling and the 'Smuggler's Song' (Students' Book, pp. 70–71) to introduce the idea that this sort of crime would not have been uncommon in villages such as the one invented. The class set up the inn again with the brief that on this particular evening a shipment of contraband will be arriving. Everyone will have a place to be and a job to do in order to ensure the safe (and profitable) passage of the goods through the village. Set the students the task of organising themselves in readiness for the shipment. At the key moment, you arrive at the inn, in role as a stranger. How do the villagers deal with this?

26 Freeze the scene; in role, reveal that you are in fact a customs officer and that a regiment of soldiers is in place at strategic points around the village, having been tipped off about the contraband. Insist that, unless the villagers reveal the identity of the local man who is the key to this black market, the inn will be torn down. What do the villagers do?

You might let this run on in a period of dramatic play or ask the students, out of role, what they think would have happened next.

27 Show the class the pictures of gibbets (Students' Book, pp. 14–15).
   (a) If the class have suggested that the key organiser of the smuggling operation was caught, narrate how he or she was hanged and gibbeted by the roadside. The whole village gathered at the foot of the gibbet on the day he or she was hauled up. In turn, students say what their relationship was to the person and perhaps what the execution has meant to them.
   (b) The class may have devised some means of ridding themselves of the customs officer. In this case, narrate how the incident signalled the end of the business and how it would only be a matter of time before the soldiers came back. Again, the group gathers at the gibbet and speaks aloud its thoughts about what the future might hold.

28 Following either of the options above, announce, in role as a young villager, that as far as you can see the village is finished. The wealth of the village depended on the trade brought from the road travel and the smuggling. Following the incident, coaches will no longer stop at the inn; the sight of the newly-erected gibbet will give them more reason to hurry through. Even more ominous is the rumour that a canal will soon be built to link London and Bristol. The best thing for the young people to do will be to leave and find a new job, perhaps helping

to build the canal or as servants in the homes of those merchants who will get rich through the trade the canal will carry. Ask students to write down what thoughts their chosen character would have about the situation. In groups, they use their jottings as the basis for a *presentation* which communicates the different reactions.

29 Still in role as the young person, tell the class that there is a stage-coach bound for London passing through at 6 am the next morning. It will stop at the milestone – the place where all the coaches stop now since the inn was accused of being in league with smugglers. The village was a nice place to be as a child, but it will be a rotten place to live in as an adult; you, for one, will take the coach and leave.

30 The students meet in groups to discuss whether or not they too will leave.

31 Out of role, refer the class back to the picture of the figure by the milestone (Students' Book, p.20). The class discuss who the figure is and what his or her connection with the village might be.

Read the passage from *The Driftway* (Students' Book, pp. 18–19) and ask the group to brainstorm what 'extra hard bit of living' might have stamped this apparition to this spot.

32 Remind the class that the drama started with them in role as young people on a day trip. *Forum theatre* is used to explore ways of providing a satisfying end to the drama which shows how the journey that day changed the people on the coach forever.

STRUCTURE B: MAPPING OUT NEW STORIES

Aims

- To encourage the imaginative construction of alternative fictions from existing narrative units.
- To make explicit the potential for restructuring narratives according to alternative viewpoints.
- To create and develop dramatic characters in the context of a chronological narrative sequence of events.
- To highlight the sense of audience in the presentation of dramatic narratives.

This structure takes the narrative units of the Students' Book and employs a range of strategies through which the students can reshape these units into their own original narrative sequences. This may well include the construction of new characters and events which will draw upon students' knowledge of the eighteenth-century context.

Finally, the structure will focus on the demands of presenting such work, and present students with the demands of a real audience.

1   Before the students begin the task of mapping their own texts, the journal itself can be reviewed as a starting point. In many ways this is a single chronological narrative which could be mapped on a straight line from point A (London) to point B (Bath), but the opportunities for narrative depth need to be highlighted.

2   Ask students to *brainstorm* as many details as they can relating to the heroine's journey. Can they remember all the people she met on the way? (Students could initially do this in pairs.) If necessary, and if the students require it, the journal could be read again from the Students' Book.

3   The narrative can now be split into its constituent 'vignettes' or episodes. Divide the students into small groups and give each group the task of presenting an account of a particular episode as part of a whole class oral narrative. Each episode of Our Heroine's progress could be presented in a *tableau* (or a series of *tableaux*, as in a Hogarth sequence), with an oral narration by one member of the group. You can move between the groups, in role as the heroine, to link the various episodes of the story.

4   In role as a TV director, gather the class together for a Programme Planning Meeting. A considerable sum has been put aside for a new eighteenth-century drama serial based on events taking place along an old coaching road. The students' task will be to come up with a winning plot.

    In role, the students can now inspect the map of the journal. The central narrative units can be highlighted (the gibbet, The Castle Inn at Windsor, the turnpike, etc.) and the path of the heroine through these units should be made clear. In addition, it is important to stress the solid arrows, as these denote where other characters (possibly from other stories, or on other journeys) touch fleetingly upon Our Heroine's progress, and thus raise opportunities for other stories to branch off. Where do these arrows lead us? Where have they come from?

5   Make it clear that this story provides some ideas for alternative narratives.

    In order to contextualise the work which is to follow, one starting point would be to consider the stories which the incidental characters of the journal have to tell about the road (those marked with a solid arrow on the map).

    These characters are *hot-seated* in order for the students to draw out any other possible stories they might have to tell about the road. The questions might at first focus on what these characters thought about the passengers in the coach, and what happened at those points in the journal where they came into contact with the coach.

    The questioning could then develop to explore the characters' own stories:
    • Why did the naked highwayman have to turn to such desperate measures?
    • Were there any villagers who did not come to work on the road as stonebreakers, or who deserted their posts to return to work?

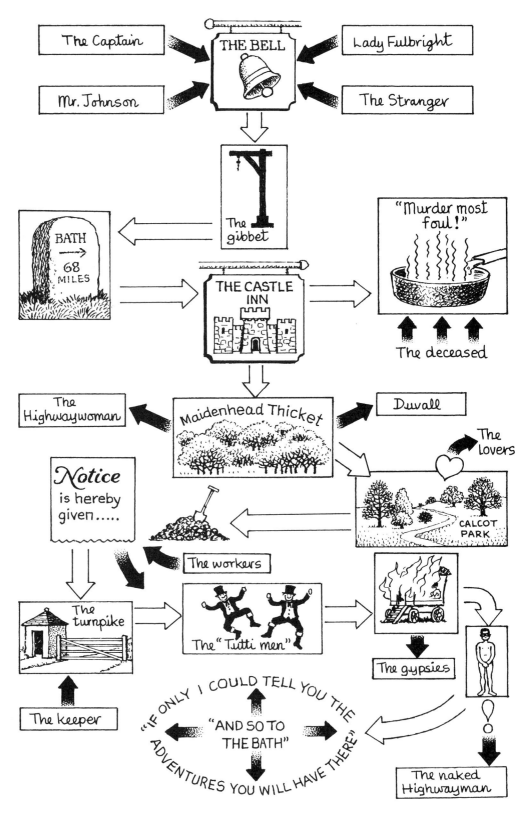

- What became of the highwaywoman?
- How did the family come to lose a relation at the gibbet?
- Has the turnpike-keeper any other tales of woe to relate about his work, or have there been events to compensate for his harsh treatment?

These conversations may well provide the links into alternative narratives of the Great Bath Road.

6 In small groups, the students, as writers, now get to work. Using the idea of mapping a narrative, they will have to map an original story which could be used for TV.

- The students can tell their new story from the viewpoint of any character they have met in the journal, or indeed from the viewpoint of a completely new character. This character must be clearly defined before the narrative work begins.
- They may use any of the resources in the Students' Book as their narrative 'units', which they can put into any order they wish. The 'units' might be a gibbet, a milestone, an inn yard – indeed any of the features of the eighteenth-century road – but the importance of the units must always be in terms of what *happened* at these places. As the units are selected, they should be drawn on to cards or pieces of paper and then placed into the right sequence as the narrative map evolves. For example:
  - The students must decide upon a narrative chain of events, and then 'map' it out on a large sheet of paper using arrows, as in the example, to link the key narrative units. Annotations should be made on to the map to explain what happens in each of these units.
  - The students can include as little, or as much, of the existing material as they wish.

On completion of the maps, each group must give a name to its story.

7 Once the maps of the new narratives have been completed, the class gather for a Planning Meeting, at which the new stories are to be presented to the Producer. Each group will be called upon to present its story to the Board, which you could chair, in role as the Producer. Encourage the class to question the plausibility of each structure. Are all the events clear? Is the sequence of events credible? Can the Board accept the characters which have been created?

8 The maps could be put up on the walls, or in a space on the floor, around the Drama space, and the groups could be given time to walk around the displays, reading the annotations and inspecting the maps in more detail.

9 Gather the groups together, again *in role* as the Producer. Inform them that all the narratives are very promising, and it has been impossible at this stage to choose between them. A further presentation will be needed to decide which story will be selected. The first scene of each narrative must be prepared and presented, so that the dramatic appeal of the story as a piece of TV drama can be assessed.

The groups will have to be briefed about the following points:

- The first 'event' or unit on their maps may not necessarily be the best starting point for the opening minutes of a TV drama. The first scene could be an event which happened before the beginning of the story (but which is connected to it in some way), or it may be the final unit of the present narrative, the rest of which will be presented as a 'flashback'. Alternatively, it could be the most dramatic moment which captures the audience's attention, with the other narrative units rearranged around it in a logical sequence.
- Reference may be made to the students' own knowledge in this area: how many 'films of the book' have they seen which change the order of the written narrative? (A good example would be to compare the opening scene of *Macbeth* with the first three minutes of the Polanski film – the students could then discuss the obvious differences, and why they have been made.)
- The visual impact of the opening scene must be foregrounded in the students' thinking. TV audiences can become distracted and will switch over if the opening scene is too tedious! How can the groups set up enigmas, mysteries, get the audience asking questions of the text?
- The groups will also need to consider the effects at their disposal: sound effects, music, a single opening image, a particular line (or no dialogue at all) could all be exploited to create tension, expectation and suspense. Reference could be made back to the enigmatic lines of the stranger in the journal (Students' Book, p.61: 'Ah yes, justice, that would be something to see on this road' and p.28: 'It pays to be well informed on this road, sir').

10 In the first instance, the outline of this scene is to be produced as a 'storyboard', in which the first 60 seconds of the story are planned as a sequence of shots in a series of chronological sketches. Each shot will need to be annotated with details of dialogue, sound and special effects to be employed, as well as information on what is happening in the story.

11 Once the storyboards have been completed, the groups will then have to consider how the remaining narrative needs to be reshaped around the opening scene: does the original map still work, or will the narrative sequence have to be reconstructed?

12 Each group rehearses its opening 60-second scene for a presentation as a 'demo'. You need to remind students that the idea here is not to tell the whole story, or to introduce all of the characters, but merely to create a powerful opening which will draw the audience into the narrative.

13 Each presentation can be followed by an explanation of where on the original narrative map each scene came from, and what changes (if any) needed to be made to the narrative to make the rest of the story work.

14 Towards the end of the journal, Lady Fullbright says to Our Heroine: 'My dear, if only I could tell you the adventures you will have there', but the story of her stay in Bath remains untold. Using 'Journey's End' tasks 2–5 (Students' Book, p.75), invite the groups to consider what might have happened to her.

15 Now refer the class back to the specimen map, where the solid arrows indicate the various options open to the heroine. Using the *mapping technique*, each group can plot a narrative covering the events of her stay in Bath. Does she come into contact again with any of the characters we have met so far? Are her adventures happy, or tragic?

16 By way of presenting these new maps, you can, in role as the heroine, stand at the centre of the space, with the groups arranged around the edges of the room. Question each group in turn as to your future; what will happen to you if you take a particular narrative path? What can each group tell you about what is to befall you? If necessary, you can call upon a group to act out a vision of your future, rather like Scrooge watching the ghost of Christmas future. How will Our Heroine react to what she sees?

STRUCTURE C: 'AN ACTOR'S LIFE FOR ME!'

Aims:

- To explore the theatrical traditions and methods of the eighteenth century and recognise their effect on modern theatre.
- To consider attitudes towards women in the theatre then and now.
- To develop technical skills appropriate to the production and performance of a piece of drama.

1 Pin a large notice to the door of the classroom, a photocopy of p. 64.

2 The class read the notice. Welcome the applicants, in role as Mrs Crummles. The following points are woven into her introduction:

- She has been in the theatrical profession all her life. (To paraphrase Dickens: 'I am in the theatrical profession myself, my husband was in the theatrical profession, my children are in the theatrical profession. I had a dog that lived and died in it from a puppy.')
- Her mother was one of the first actresses to appear on an English stage (the very first one being in 1660).
- She set up the company with her husband some years ago, and they have been touring through times rough and smooth ever since.
- The new show will open *here* at The Bell in The Strand and play in inns along the Bath Road.
- At present, the company's entire possessions are stored and transported in a wagon, but she is certain (as always) that the new show is sure to bring in sufficient money for her to buy and establish a theatre in Bath.

3 Mrs Crummles invites applicants to tell each other and her about what has drawn them to a life in the theatre. Perhaps they have seen companies at work, or perhaps they have no other work themselves. Perhaps they have left home in search of fame and fortune . . .

NOTICE

To all would-be Thespians,
Actors, Players, Singers, Songsters, Troubadours and
Craftsmen of Theatrical Persuasion.

The Honourable and Established Company of
Strolling Players
known here and elsewhere as

Mrs Crummles' Company

is this day seeking recruits
for the purpose of presenting a new play,
for presentation in respectable houses and inns
along
The Great Bath Road,
this coming season
1770

Apply within to
Mrs Vincent Crummles

(The character of Mrs Crummles is taken from *Nicholas Nickleby*; chapters 22–24 of that book will give you an insight into the role of an actor-manager.)

In role as Mrs Crummles, support the students in this *dramatic play*, feeding in information about the plays and life of the times.

4 Mrs Crummles is anxious to find out more about the applicants: what skills might they possess which will be of use to the travelling company? The information is gathered through a *whole group role play*. Alternatively, smaller groups could jot down their skills on cards, or each applicant could be asked to draw up a brief 'curriculum vitae', outlining his or her relevant experience.

5 Out of role, invite the students to recap on the situation that has been explored so far:

- When is the drama set?
- Where is it set?
- What do they know about Mrs Crummles?
- What sort of people are applying to be in her company?
- What have they learned about the theatre at that time?

6 Ask the class to explore the last question further by working in groups and *brainstorming* what differences there might be between the way plays were presented in the eighteenth century and the way they are presented now. (You may choose to give some headings to prompt discussion, for example lighting, sound effects, scenery, costumes, make-up.)

Discuss where plays were put on and who would have watched them.

7 The class reconsider their work in **4** above and divide into groups of 'experts' on the different skills required. Students are set the task of *researching* how their particular skill would have been used in the eighteenth-century theatre. This sort of project work will be used to support the tasks laid out below. You could suggest that students become 'experts' on: scenery; props; costume; lighting; sound effects; script writing. (The class may need to be reassured that all members will be called upon to play numerous parts in the rehearsals of the play.)

8 In role again as Mrs Crummles, introduce the subject of the play that the company will present: the romantic adventures of a young lady journeying from London to Bath for the first time. The trouble is that the script currently exists only in the form of a fictitious journal with a most unsatisfactory ending, which presents a string of problems as regards the staging of the play! By way of example, ask the class to read Chapter One of the journal in the Students' Book (pp. 6–7).

In role as the newly assembled company, the students discuss the problems of putting this chapter on *any* stage, let alone their small touring one. The different groups make notes on which problems they will need to consider further.

9 Mrs Crummles expresses doubts about the way Our Heroine is depicted; she seems a little dull and weak. By referring to task **3** (Students' Book, p.8), the company uses *hot-seating* to build a stronger character. Students find an appropriate name for the heroine and list three particular qualities she possesses. (Make a note of these, as they will be needed later on.)

10 The newly-constructed heroine is put to the test in a rehearsal of how she meets her fellow passengers for the first time (see task **5**, Students' Book, p.10). *Forum theatre* is used to explore the different ways of playing the character and the effect each one would have on an audience. How would the actress playing her ensure that the three qualities (noted in **9**, above) were shown? The company considers appropriate lines, gestures and expressions for her which will suggest these qualities.

11 Mrs Crummles desires that the teams of experts consider some particular problems in the rest of the journal. You may, of course, just ask them to read through all the journal entries in the mantle of their chosen expert. The notes below might be used as a guide to the problems that will need to be solved:

Scenery
General constraints
Scenery has to be transported and must therefore be kept to a minimum. The play will be performed in some quite small rooms, on the floor or on small raised stages, possibly out of doors. Choose bits of furniture which could be used in several different scenes. Can any pieces of scenery be made to fold up? Could painted backcloths (which may be rolled up) be used?

Tasks
- List, sketch or find pictures of the different locations mentioned in the journal.
- List, sketch or find pictures of the *essential* pieces of stage furniture, for example chairs, tables, beds, etc.
- List and sketch any painted backcloths you want to use.
- Draw a design showing how a larger piece of scenery might be made to fold up.

Props
General constraints
Props will be needed to suggest locations and character types. None of the props can be very valuable (though they might appear to be).

Tasks
- List, sketch or find pictures of the 'personal' props the main characters will need.
- List, sketch or find pictures of *essential* properties which will help set some of the scenes, for example candlesticks, plates, bottles, etc.

Costumes
General constraints
The play is set in 1770 so appropriate costumes wouldn't have been very difficult for Mrs Crummles' Company to find. What should a company working 200 years later look for? In the eighteenth century, there was a great danger of some costumes catching fire on stage because of the way places used to be lit – would this be a problem today?

Tasks
- Sketch or find pictures of appropriate costumes for the main characters.
- Find out what fabrics were used at the time. Would they be available to modern companies? What alternatives might a modern company use?
- Would any of the characters need costume changes? How could such changes be simplified?

Lighting
General constraints
In 1770, candles or oil lamps would have provided the lighting (gas light wasn't used until 1816). Different colours could be achieved by placing stained glass in front of the light source, but it was difficult to focus light or to change the intensity of it. How could a company today create an 'authentic' atmosphere by using modern electric lights?

Tasks
- Look carefully at the type of light produced by a candle, an oil lamp and a modern stage light. Note the differences and see if you can make the modern light look more like the others.
- Consult the stage design team to find out what different locations will need to be lit.
- Jot down the number of lights and colours you will use for the different scenes. Pay particular attention to the differences between indoors and outdoors, day and night.
- Make up a cue sheet to show your ideas clearly.
- Jot down ideas for some special effects which modern electric lights might allow, for example, projecting rainfall or flickering firelight.

Sound effects
General constraints
Today, audio tape is generally used for sound effects, and companies sometimes use voices and musical instruments imaginatively to create appropriate effects. In 1770, various mechanical devices would have been used to create effects such as wind and thunder. (At Bristol Old Vic, a wooden chute zig-zagged down from the top of the building to the cellars. Cannon balls were rolled down to create an impression of thunder.) Mrs Crummles' Company would have to have been very imaginative if it wished to devise any sound effects.

Tasks
- List all the effects which you would wish to use in the play.
- Experiment with voices, instruments and other ways of making sounds to see if they can be recreated.
- Find out what sound effects are available on record from the library.
- Tape-record a sequence of effects which captures the sound of the coach leaving a busy inn and setting off down a road.

Script writing

General constraints

Writing a complete playscript from the journal would be a huge task. Students wanting to tackle script writing would benefit from the work suggested in **Structure B: Mapping Out New Stories.**

Tasks

- Pick out the *essential* pieces of action in the journal.
- Note down any lines of dialogue in the journal which you would want to keep in the play.
- Invent a line or two for each of the main characters which they might repeat from time to time; a personal expression or saying.
- Choose one scene in which you think the heroine appears to be quite a weak character. Mrs Crummles wants the heroine to appear more interesting, so write the scene in such a way that she shows the three qualities decided on in **9** above.
- Mrs Crummles is dissatisfied with the way the journal ends. Write a new scene which you think will make the end of Our Heroine's journey more satisfactory.

12 Decide on the most appropriate way for groups to present their work.

- One option would be to tie it all together and actually rehearse and perform the play that Mrs Crummles' Company takes on tour.
- Alternatively, the class present their work in terms of a museum display. Students could use models, drawings and pieces of descriptive or documentary writing, together with extracts from the script which arose from the journal, to show how Mrs Crummles' Company would have presented the play.

13 Another option would be to continue the practical drama in terms of a period *Noises Off* backstage area. Here, the company must deal with a number of the adventures encountered on its journey from London to Bath. This might involve tackling the following sections of the Students' Book in role as the company:

- 'Travel Games', pp. 17–18: how do the members of the company amuse themselves as they walk behind their wagon from one venue to another?
- 'Highwaywomen', pp. 32–3: the company is held up by a highwaywoman (an opportunity here to use a second *teacher-in-role*?). How does it try to avoid handing over the hard earned takings from its last performance?
- 'Turnpikes and their Keepers', pp. 46–9: the company encounters a difficult turnpike-keeper. What tactics does it employ, as a group of entertainers, to try and appease him?
- 'Misery and Hazard', pp. 65–7: the company's wagon is overturned when it runs into a flooded pot hole.

14 The drama is used to tackle the issue of equal opportunities when the father of the actress playing the heroine turns up. He demands that she return home with him, on the grounds that acting is an unsuitable vocation for a young woman.

- The class use *imaging* to portray what they think the popular idea of life as an actress might have been at the time.
- Students *hot-seat* the father and the actress in order to try and find out why she left home in the first place.
- *Forum theatre* is used to explore possible outcomes. Groups represent the actress, Mrs Crummles and the father in a meeting.
- Small groups form contrasting *tableaux* to show what they think the future will be like for the actress, depending on whether she stays with the company or leaves it.
- The class consider why there appear to be so few women playwrights, directors or actor-managers in the history of English theatre. Students carry out research into some of the women we do know about in pre-nineteenth-century theatre, for example Aphra Behn, Sarah Siddons, Peg Woffington, Nell Gwynne. It is worth noting that, at the start of the eighteenth century (when the fictitious mother of our Mrs Crummles would have been at work), almost one half of all new plays produced in London were written by women; who were the playwrights, and why have their plays been so ignored?

15 A notable figure in the theatre world of the eighteenth century was the critic R. B. Sheridan (who lived in Bath). He satirised the self-importance of these writers in his play *The Critic* (1779).

On arrival in Bath, Mrs Crummles' Company is promised a loan which will enable it to set up a playhouse if it can produce a set of 'notices' regarding its play. After explaining the nature and purpose of a theatre review and looking at some modern examples (perhaps from local newspapers on school productions), the students write the reviews of the Crummles' Company play for presentation to the potential benefactor.

(Should they be complimentary enough to allow the company to set up its own playhouse, the class will presumably have another drama project on their hands, investigating what eighteenth-century theatres looked like and deciding what the first production in Mrs Crummles' theatre should be!)

R e s o u r c e s

The notes below pertain to the individual activities in the Pupils' Book.

Introduction (pp. 1–2)

1 Display
Whole class
Objective: To gather and share experiences.

The historical setting of the resource material is likely to be unfamiliar to most students. By starting the work in the students' own experiences, the move into the era is eased. The display also presents opportunities for group co-operation and gives each student's contribution an importance. The format of the display will allow it to grow and develop over the weeks spent on this project.

2 Imaging
Groups: 3–5   15 mins
Objective: To focus on visual elements of narrative.

The exercise immediately suggests the idea of character development. Sometimes, viewing images like this can become a guessing game for the rest of the class. Try allowing the audience to question people in the image about who they are and what has happened.

3 Telegram
Individuals   20 mins
Objective: To encourage students to use language sparingly and accurately in an appropriate context.

Although it suggests in the Students' Book that students write a poem based on a few carefully chosen words, other options would be to write (in role as a harassed traveller) a telegram or postcard on arrival at a destination, capturing the change that the character feels has taken place to himself or herself.

4 Research
Whole class

The information collected in order to make the display (task **1**) would serve as a useful starting point for this kind of research. You will find some useful advice about how to get students to formulate appropriate questions for this kind of work on p.64 of *Evacuees*.

Paths That Cross (pp. 3–5)

1 Deduction
Whole class

Encourage the class to speculate about 'evidence' like this. The idea that somehow things past have left an indelible mark on the present is an important aspect of this book and may be effective for three reasons. First, it may encourage students to look at their own surroundings more carefully for evidence of the past. Secondly, it may trigger their imagination (the idea that the past might start to affect people in the present is a recurring theme in Penelope Lively's books for children). Thirdly, the idea that each of us is the result of all that has gone before is an important one which allows us to understand the effect we may have on the future.

2 Improvisation
Pairs   5 mins
Objective: To engage in dramatic play.

One way of organising this task would be to get the students into pairs, read the extract aloud and then simply tell them to carry on. The extract is a good foundation for spontaneous improvisation, and the students' work will enhance their ability to speculate about the content and meaning of the piece.

3 Creative Writing
Individuals

Most, if not all, students will know of a local abandoned house or building about which stories abound, and will be motivated to talk about it. As with any creative subject, the teacher's job often involves trying to channel that motivation into something tangible and concrete which can be shaped and shared.

4 Creative Writing
Individuals/pairs

As a variation on the usual individually-produced creative writing task, try to offer alternatives, for example:
- You are a *pair* of investigative journalists who have been looking into a local event or phenomenon. Write your story for the local paper.
- One of you is an interviewer for a local radio station, the other an amateur psychic researcher. Write the transcript of (or record on cassette) a short interview between the two of you which was broadcast.

The Season At Bath (pp. 7–8)

I Mime/Movement
Groups: 2–6   20 mins
Objective: To use a range of movements and gestures to depict images appropriate to the narrative.

The idea of a 'dramatised dream' can be a very liberating one – after all, anything can happen in a dream. Referring to the fragmentary nature of dreams can also encourage students to break away from the linear naturalism of most televisual drama and persuade them to experiment with time and space more imaginatively.

DEVELOPMENT (2)
                                                                                          20 mins

At this point in the narrative, the students know very little about either Our Heroine or the historical period. Rather than discussing this before setting task **1**, invite the class to question anything which they see in each other's work which they feel *might* be anachronistic.

Record these questions and refer to them when setting up task **2**. This task should be done quite quickly, with the intention of sharing vernacular knowledge and raising questions about the period which can be researched later.

3 Hot-Seating
Whole class   10 mins
Objective: To develop a dramatic character consistent with information available.

This is a further development of the tasks above. It introduces the cental figure of Our Heroine, moving the students to consider a personal story rather than an historical study.

Coaching Days (pp. 9–10)

I Design
Individuals   15 mins

Making 'WANTED' posters is a popular activity, but one which is rarely developed beyond a superficial jokiness. In this context, students might be introduced to works by Hogarth and Rowlandson and invited to consider how they might use make-up to achieve the grotesque caricatures. Displaying the drawings is simply a way of marking an idea. Stress that these designs are being made in order to develop ideas which will be used in the drama; they will not be assessed in terms of the draftsmanship they exhibit.

2 Design
Whole class   10 mins
Objective: To develop spatial awareness.

3 Soundscape/Thought-Tracking
Whole group
Objectives: To develop sense of space, atmosphere and character through sound
                alone.
                To deepen commitment to character.

The tasks in this section build gradually on each other. Careful structuring is needed here in order to avoid the superficial. Using narration as you walk around the courtyard will help students build their own mental image and help them to contract into the drama; comment on what people appear to be doing, what they look like, what the courtyard smells like.

4 Improvisation
Pairs   5 mins
Objective: To portray characters with conviction.

Before setting this task, invite the students to decide whether they want to bring 'real' characters alive in this courtyard or whether they would like to try and breathe life into the sort of caricatures depicted by Hogarth. This will mean discussing to some extent *why* Hogarth depicted people like this; was he simply being cruel or was he telling us something about the times in which he lived? The ensuing improvisations can be evaluated in terms of the extent to which the *form* clearly affects the way we understand the *content*.

5 Role-On-The-Wall/Small Group Work
Groups: 3–5   20 mins
Objective: To contruct and portray a rounded dramatic character.

Draw the groups' attention to the way in which the key to dramatic characters, particularly from this era, can be found in their names. Examples are: **Pinchwife** and **Sir Jasper Fidget** from *The Country Wife* by William Wycherley; **Mr Worthy** and **Captain Brazen** from *The Recruiting Officer* by George Farquhar; **Tony Lumpkin** and **Mr Hardcastle** from *She Stoops to Conquer* by Oliver Goldsmith.

(You might decide *not* to mention **Dolly Spanker** from Boucicault's *London Assurance*, however!)

The class might like to speculate on what Our Heroine's name could be before starting this exercise.

6 Improvisation
Groups: 4–5
Objective: To adapt to a variety of dramatic roles.

One way of organising this scene would be to remix the groups from task **5**. In this way, students could bring more informed characters to the new improvisation. If the scenes are shared, the class might evaluate the way individuals translated their characters in the new situations.

7 Creative Writing
Individuals

Crime And Punishment (pp. 12–15)

1 Discussion
Groups: 3–6   5 mins
Objective: To work towards deepening the students' concept of the dramatic.

Many groups will offer ideas which are action-orientated and shallow. Ask each group about the coherence of its ideas: for example, if the man was hanged for being a mass murderer, why does the horseman appear to show such respect? Without being overtly judgemental, try to steer the students away from seeing the character in one-dimensional terms; suggest they consider, for example, the man's family situation or how he treated his friends.

The tasks in this section all deal with ways of deepening the way students construct dramatic characters. Following through all of the tasks in sequence would, therefore, be more useful than dipping into them at random.

2 and 3 Improvisation
Small groups   40 mins
Objective: To explore the dramatic potential of personal relationships.

One particularly useful option here would be to use *forum theatre* techniques to explore some of the students' improvisations. Give each group 10 minutes to devise a scene showing the last meeting between the hanged man and the other two figures. Ask one group to show its work and invite the audience to suggest other ways of playing the same scene by changing some aspect of the characters, particular lines or the timing, etc. Sharing ideas in this way will inevitably raise the question of what the intention of the scene is: do the students want the scene to be sad, mysterious, exciting? After 10 minutes of this sort of discussion, give groups the chance to re-inspect their improvisations and tighten the focus.

The next task should show a coherent development of the narrative and characters.

4 Improvisation
Pairs   5 mins
Objective: To focus on the nature and dramatic potential of dialogue.

As with tasks **1–3**, initial responses in the practical exercise might be superficial. One way of deepening the work would be to encourage pairs to script the improvisation and, in doing so, edit and reshape their ideas.

5 Hot-Seating/Tableau
Whole group/small groups   25 mins
Objectives: To explore the way in which different dramatic characters may be constructed from a given stimulus.
To demonstrate an understanding of how characters might have a three-dimensional quality.

Ask the three volunteers to sit in different corners of the room. The investigating groups may then move from one to another, taking note of the different responses as they move around.

As a whole group, share responses on how the volunteers physically demonstrated their different characters and how this matched what they were saying.

For part (**b**), comment on the dramatic power of showing an unexpected side to a character.

6 and 7 Improvisation/Creative Writing
Groups: 2–4/individuals   20 mins
Objective: To consolidate the work on creating three-dimensional characters by using a variety of dramatic forms.

8 Improvisation
Groups: 2–6/individuals   20 mins
Objective: To develop a dramatic narrative through appropriate discussion and rehearsal.

The nature of this task invites students to respond in a more action-orientated way. You may need to make the comment that people can still be shown as having different sides to their character even in action/horror stories.

Travel Games (pp. 17–18)

1 and 2 Research
Pairs
Objective: To encourage use of dictionaries and quick reference to extend
knowledge of language and literature.

3 Game
Pairs   10 mins
Objective: To encourage students to 'play' with language.

Students are often extremely good at spotting and using double meanings. This
exercise empowers them to play with language in a more productive way.

4 Improvisation
Groups: 3–5   10 mins
Objective: To show an understanding of dramatic tension.

As an introduction to this exercise, you might consider how different games have
moments of great tension: for example, as a whole group, play 'Granny's Footsteps'
or 'What's the Time, Mr Wolf?' and then ask the class to isolate the moment of
greatest tension. How can students use this idea of a tense moment in a scene of
their own?

Milestones (pp. 18–20)

1 and 2 Imaging
Groups: 2–4   10 mins
Objective: To use visual images to communicate an idea.

3 and 4 Creative Writing
Individuals

5 Hot-Seating
Whole group   5 mins
Objective: To create a dramatic character.

This exercise enables the students to share ideas and build a foundation for their
work in task **6**.

6 Telegram
Individuals/whole group   5 mins
Objective: To use language or movement economically.

This task could be converted into a game which develops an awareness of
movement. Two or three volunteers stand out, while the rest of the class adopt the
position of the figure in the photograph. The game is that, when the volunteers start
to walk around the room, they will make a number of actions; scratching their nose,
stroking their hair, etc. Each of the 'statues' will have previously decided on an
action which will be the trigger which brings him or her to life. The volunteers must
try to identify which action brings each statue to life; if they do so successfully, the

statue joins them to try and catch the others. The students could also use words rather than actions as triggers.

7 Small Group
Groups: 3–6   30 mins
Objective: To develop a dramatic narrative and an appropriate form through discussion and rehearsal.

Murder Most Foul (pp. 22–4)

I–5 Class Play
Whole class   1½ hrs
Objectives: To create, organise and re-enact a linear dramatic narrative in an appropriate genre. To discuss different styles of presentation in an historical context.

This authentic 'murder mystery' may offer the class teacher the opportunity to draw a number of elements of the students' work together. The tasks suggested in the Students' Book may be tackled one by one by the whole class or simultaneously by different groups. You may wish to work in role as a senior investigator, guiding assistant detectives in their tasks and helping to question key witnesses.

(*a*) In addition to drawing a ground plan of the inn, try marking out different rooms on the hall/studio floor with tape or string. In role as the senior detective, take the class on a tour of the inn, introducing each room and asking students to add any details which might be significant (these should be recorded on a card and left in the room). For example:

> And here, ladies and gentlemen, is the kitchen. Notice the open door into the back yard and this stack of as yet unwashed copper pans. Look around you. What else do you notice about the décor and organisation of this room?

The picture on p.25 (*Old Bull and Mouth Inn*) may be used to assist this task.

(*b*) An alternative to a simple listing of characters would be to ask each member of the class to simulate one particular document identifying a character present: for example, some kind of passbook, a letter of introduction, a share certificate, etc. You could mount these on a display board and invite the whole class, in role as detectives, to write comments next to them which point out significant details. The list of employees on p.24 is a useful resource to support this task.

(*c*) The following brief details might be copied and given to volunteers who take the parts of the four key witnesses:

LUCY

Has worked for Mrs Partridge, the landlady, for two months. She is the eldest girl in her family and in charge of a number of smaller brothers and sisters (her mother is dead and her father in prison for bad debts). She is very obedient and anxious to keep her job. Sometimes Mrs Partridge tells her to do things she doesn't like, but she is afraid to speak openly against her mistress. The day before the deaths, she made a pan of turtle soup ready for the meeting of the Colnbrook Turnpike Trust, but Mrs Partridge called on her to prepare some rooms before she had finished the job. On the day of the deaths, she saw Mr Burcombe in the kitchens. Although he dined on beef, he was freely tasting the dishes left over from the meal eaten by the rest of the Trustees.

MR POTE

Mr Pote is a very fussy man and suspicious of everyone and everything. He doesn't enjoy the company of his fellow Trustees and certainly doesn't enjoy the company of the poor. On the fateful morning, the local magistrates ordered a number of paupers, who were not local men, to return to their own parishes for help. A group of them stopped at The Castle to beg for food for their journey. Pote suggests that they may have spread a dreadful infection. During the morning, Pote was also horrified to see a group of felons stopping at the inn – goodness only knows what evil plans they may have had for the respectable members of the Trust! Distressed by all this, Pote took a walk. On his return, he picked over his lunch, most of it not being to his liking.

DR JAMES

Dr James was the first to examine the victims and found a number of curious things. Major Mayne, for one, clearly had an infection which was several days' old, while Captain O'Brian was a notorious drinker and probably just suffered from too much port. Dr James examined the pauper named James Jackson that morning on behalf of the local magistrates who had ordered him out of the town. The man was simply half starved. Dr James also knew full well that one of the people Jackson was supposed to have infected had been seriously ill for the last nine years, while the other one was well over eighty years old anyway! Dr James was certain that the cause of the illness and deaths was some kind of food poisoning.

MRS PARTRIDGE

Mrs Partridge frequently boasts of running the best inn in Windsor. She certainly makes a good living from the business. Mrs Partridge is keen to look after her 'better' customers, such as the men from the Turnpike Trust for whom she had ordered a special turtle soup to be made. Though she would be reluctant to admit it to others, she sometimes cuts corners in order to make a profit. For example, she had hurried Lucy away to clean some rooms on the previous day, leaving the turtle soup in the copper pan rather than transferring it into the earthenware tureen.

(*d*) Yes, you've got it! It was the turtle soup that did for them! Left standing overnight in the copper pan, it had been tainted with verdigris. The mystery went on for years until Mrs Partridge finally admitted her knowledge of this on her deathbed. You may choose to ignore this and pursue the suggestions of the class. However, it is also interesting to reveal this actual fact to the students and then carefully construct the suggested scenes so that the real reason emerges from a number of other possibilities. The 'mapping' device explained in

Structure B could be used here, and a number of scenes created, placed into an appropriate order and represented as a coherent (though embryonic) play. This small project should offer the teacher the opportunity to introduce knowledge about genres such as the thriller or documentary drama.

(e) Groups are likely to come up with far more bizarre and intricate plots than the historical truth. Talk about how a good 'murder mystery' story works: its tightness of plot, neatness of construction and the gradual unfolding of the events from a number of red herrings.

Inns (pp. 24-7)

I Tableau/Narration

Groups: 4–6   20 mins

Objective: To use a variety of dramatic forms to convey an idea.

The purpose of this exercise is that, having devised a simple narrative, the students select its key elements and find appropriate, economical ways of illustrating them in a series of tableaux; the process is the same as devising a storyboard. In addition to making the tableaux, the class will need to experiment with ways of telling the story verbally. When groups share their work, ask the audience to consider what elements of the story could only be told in words and what was most effectively conveyed in pictures.

2 Creative Writing

3 Improvisation

Groups: 3–5   15 mins

Objective: To develop a piece of drama through appropriate discussion and
             rehearsal.

It is worth discussing the nature of the examples given. Some could be seen as irreverent, perhaps even offensive. There may be some dramatic mileage in the idea of the landlord exploiting some historical incident to attract tourists and then getting his comeuppance!

4 Rolling Role

Whole group   1½ hrs

Objective: To explore the dramatic developments possible from a given situation.

The concept of the 'rolling role' is that material generated by one group is taken up and developed by another. In this particular exercise, the work is developed in stages. You may, initially, ask the students to adopt a frozen image of their chosen character in a pose which suggests a typical action. A few members of the group might be asked to describe what they are doing, wearing or thinking in their frozen situation. You activate the still images by clapping; each time you clap, students find a new partner and improvise a few lines which reflect their character. Having built a range of characters to be involved in the drama, consider the suggestions for a starting point in the Students' Book. Each one provides a role for the teacher as the instigator of a drama. Having launched the idea, give control of the work over to the students. One way of doing this would be to divide the class into small groups which then take it in turns to decide on the starting point for the next scene.

Two Gentlemen Of The Road (pp. 30–31)

1 Meeting/Creative Writing
Whole group   10 mins
Objective: To sustain a dramatic role.

You might usefully act as a chairperson in this activity. Rather than challenging statements directly, invite the students themselves to offer counter-arguments. Try to make the decision difficult for them by insisting that the implications and consequences of each suggestion are explored thoroughly. The greater the complexity of the argument, the more difficult but rewarding the ultimate statement to the newspaper will be (this may, of course, be set as an individual or small group task).

2 Monologue
Individuals/pairs
Objective: To write for a particular dramatic form/employ vocal skills to portray a character.

Insisting that students learn a monologue and then present it formally would seem to be a frighteningly intimidating, and thus unproductive, thing to do. However, introducing students to the dramatic form of monologue simply extends their knowledge of Drama and offers opportunities to those who wish to experiment with it practically. In this particular case, some fun could be had by presenting Captain Hind as a melodramatic hero declaiming away. The comedy of this is easily contrasted with the reality of the situation already touched on in the section on 'Crime and Punishment' (Students' Book, p.12).

3 Creative Writing
Groups: 2–4   30 mins
Objective: To use an appropriate style of language.

If students have access to desk top publishing facilities, this sort of task can be developed to meet a number of other National Curriculum requirements regarding IT and Media Education.

4 Meeting
Whole group   15 mins
Objective: To sustain a dramatic role/discuss different styles of presentation.

The content of such a meeting as this might be interesting enough in itself, but, by raising questions about genre stereotyping and hero worship, the scenario presents an interesting formal problem: how could a group generate dramatic tension by suggesting a crowd outside which is threatening those meeting inside? Options include: the use of sound effects or strategically placed lines of dialogue, or breaking naturalistic conventions by using tableaux and direct address (speaking the demonstrators' thoughts aloud, for example).

Highwaywomen (pp. 32–3)

1–4 Improvisation
Groups: 3–5   15 mins
Objective: To identify some of the different elements that make up a drama.

One of the elements of Drama as we see it is 'discourse': the drama says something to an audience. In the suggestions for improvisation offered here, it would be interesting to investigate what the different scenes say about women and attitudes to women. Is the idea of a highwaywoman ridiculous? Comical? Disorientating? Challenging? The construction of Our Heroine follows a deliberate stereotype – the one suggested by romantic literature. But is there another type of woman and, if so, what has made her (*a*) different from Our Heroine and (*b*) more of a rarity in English literature and common perception? These questions might appear difficult and complex, but simply asking the class to consider how different groups are presenting women in their improvisations will provide a way-in to these important issues.

Popular Heroes (pp. 33–6)

Alfred Noyes' poem 'The Highwayman' is a magnificent example of the way the 'gentlemen of the road' have been mythologised. It is reproduced on the next four pages in its entirety and may be photocopied for use with the students. Its strong rhythms and lilting imagery are quintessentially romantic.

PRESENTATION
Groups: 4–6   30 mins
Objective: To increase awareness of rhythm, pace, pitch and volume.

For good reasons, the practice of having students recite poems by heart has been abandoned in most schools. An important objection to this activity was that it was often imposed on a class without allowing the students either to grapple with the meaning of the poem or to experiment freely with the different effects which might be achieved by using a range of vocal skills.

Following the **Questions to talk and think about** (Students' Book, p.33), ask groups to discuss the following questions:

• What is the basic story of the poem?
• Could it be a 'true' story?
• If it was true, has the poet reported it as fact, or has he focused on particular parts of the story?
• With whom does the poet want us to sympathise?

THE HIGHWAYMAN

by Alfred Noyes

Part One

THE wind was a torrent of darkness among the gusty
      trees.
The moon was a ghostly galleon tossed upon cloudy
      seas.
The road was a ribbon or moonlight over the purple
      moor,
And the highwayman came riding—
      Riding—Riding—
The highwayman came riding, up to the old inn-
      door.
He'd a French cocked-hat on his forehead, a bunch
      of lace at his chin.
A coat of the claret velvet, and breeches of brown
      doe-skin.
They fitted with never a wrinkle. His boots were up
      to the thigh.
And he rode with a jewelled twinkle,
      His pistol butts a-twinkle,
His rapier hilt a-twinkle, under the jewelled sky.

Over the cobbles he clattered and clashed in the dark
      inn-yard.
He tapped with his whip on the shutters, but all
      was locked and barred.
He whistled a tune to the window, and who should be
      waiting there
But the landlord's black-eyed daughter,
      Bess, the landlord's daughter,
Plaiting a dark red love-knot into her long black hair.

And dark in the dark old inn-yard a stable-wicket
      creaked
Where Tim the ostler listened. His face was white
      and peaked.
His eyes were hollows of madness, his hair like mouldy
      hay,
But he loved the landlord's daughter,
      The landlord's red-lipped daughter.
Dumb as a dog he listened, and he heard the robber
      say—
"One kiss, my bonny sweetheart I'm after a prize
      to-night,

But I shall be back with the yellow gold before the
        morning light;
Yet, if they press me sharply, and harry me through
        the day,
Then look for me by moonlight,
        Watch for me by moonlight,
I'll come to thee by moonlight, though hell should
        bar the way."

He rose upright in the stirrups. He scarce could
        reach her hand,
But she loosened her hair i' the casement. His face
        burnt like a brand
As the black cascade of perfume came tumbling over
        his breast;
And he kissed its waves in the moonlight,
        (Oh, sweet black waves in the moonlight!)
Then he tugged at his rein in the moonlight, and
        galloped away to the west.

PART TWO

He did not come in the dawning. He did not come at
        noon;
And out o' the tawny sunset, before the rise o' the
        moon,
When the road was a gipsy's ribbon, looping the
        purple moor,
A red-coat troop came marching—
        Marching—marching—
King George's men came marching, up to the old inn-
        door.

They said no word to the landlord. They drank his
        ale instead.
But they gagged his daughter, and bound her, to the
        foot of her narrow bed.
Two of them knelt at her casement, with muskets at
        their side!
There was death at every window;
        And hell at one dark window;
For Bess could see, through her casement, the road
        that *he* would ride.

They had tied her up to attention, with many a
        sniggering jest.
They had bound a musket beside her, with the
        muzzle beneath her breast!

"Now, keep good watch!" and they kissed her.
       She heard the dead man say —
Look for me by moonlight;
       Watch for me by moonlight;
I'll come to thee by moonlight, though hell should bar the
       way!

She twisted her hands behind her; but all the knots
       held good!
She writhed her hands till her fingers were wet with
       sweat or blood!
They stretched and strained in the darkness, and
       the hours crawled by like years,
Till, now, on the stroke of midnight,
       Cold, on the stroke of midnight,
The tip of one finger touched it! The trigger at least
       was hers!

The tip of one finger touched it. She strove no more
       for the rest.
Up, she stood up to attention, with the muzzle
       beneath her breast.
She would not risk their hearing; she would not
       strive again;
For the road lay bare in the moonlight;
       Blank and bare in the moonlight;
And the blood of her veins, in the moonlight,
       throbbed to her love's refrain.

Tlot-Tlot; tlot-tlot! Had they heard it! The
       horse-hoofs ringing clear;
Tlot-tlot, tlot-tlot, in the distance? Were they deaf
       that they did not hear?
Down the ribbon of moonlight, over the brow of the
       hill,
The highwayman came riding,
       Riding, riding!
The red-coats looked to their priming! She stood up,
       straight and still.

Tlot-tlot, in the frosty silence! *Tlot-tlot,* in the
       echoing night!
Nearer he came and nearer. Her face was like a
       light.
Her eyes grew wide for a moment; she drew one last
       deep breath.
Then her finger moved in the moonlight,
       Her musket shattered the moonlight,

Shattered her breast in the moonlight and warned
    him—with her death.

He turned. He spurred to the west; he did not
    know who stood
Bowed with her head o'er the musket, drenched
    with her own blood!
Not till the dawn he heard it, and, his face grew grey
    to hear
How Bess, the landlord's daughter,
    The landlord's black-eyed daughter,
Had watched for her love in the moonlight, and died
    in the darkness there.

Back, he spurred like a madman, shouting a curse to
    the sky,
With the white road smoking behind him and his
    rapier brandished high.
Blood-red were his spurs i' the golden noon; wine-
    red was his velvet coat,
When they shot him down on the highway,
    Down like a dog on the highway,
And he lay in his blood on the highway, with the
    bunch of lace at his throat.

       .   .   .   .

And still of a winter's night, they say, when the wind is
    in the trees,
When the moon is a ghostly galleon tossed upon cloudy
    seas,
When the road is a ribbon of moonlight over the purple
    moor,
A highwayman comes riding—
    Riding—riding—
A highwayman comes riding, up to the old inn-door.

Over the cobbles he clatters and clangs in the dark
    inn-yard.
He taps with his whip on the shutters, but all is
    locked and barred.
He whistles a tune to the window, and who should be
    waiting there
But the landlord's black-eyed daughter,
    Bess, the landlord's daughter,
Plaiting a dark red love-knot into her long black hair.

- Whom does he want us to admire?
- What does Charles Keeping's illustration add to the atmosphere and effect of the poem?

Ask groups to take one short section of the poem which they think gives the reader a particularly strong impression of one of the characters. How can they use their voices and any visual images to make sure the audience see the character in the same way that they do?

DEVELOPMENT

Some groups may wish to record sections or the whole of the poem. Another option would be to work with the whole class and develop the poem 'chorally', with vocally-produced sound effects.

- Ask the class to imagine that Alfred Noyes has been put on trial for glamorising highway robbery and encouraging others to take it up. What lines or phrases might a lawyer read out in court to make the author appear guilty of such a charge? How would the lawyer read them out?

I Presentation

Groups: 4–6   30 mins

Objectives: To identify the different elements which make up Drama.
　　　　　　　To employ vocal and movement skills to realise a non-dramatic text.

Unlike a playscript, the comic book gives its audience verbal and visual information simultaneously. A spread such as this (from Raymond Briggs' *Gentleman Jim*) gives the atmosphere and content of a complete sequence of events at one glance.

Transferring this information to the dramatic form requires the students to assimilate the '*mise en scène*' and then order the information chronologically; unlike visual art, Drama is 'temporal' – the use of time is one of its key elements.

In this extract, the romance of the Alfred Noyes poem is heightened further in order to create bathos and a feeling of sympathy for the lowly James. How can the everyday be contrasted with the heightened speech and romance of the highwayman fiction and this contrast captured by a sudden change in vocal and visual presentation?

2 Improvisation

Groups: 2–4   15 mins

Objective: To develop a stimulus within an established dramatic style.

Encourage the students to experiment with bathos. Young people tend to be familiar with the way comedy is created by anti-climax. This task gives them licence to try and manipulate the effect for themselves.

Making The Bath Road Great (pp. 39–41)

I Presentation

Groups: 4–6   20 mins

Objective: To employ vocal and movement skills to realise a piece of non-dramatic text.

2 Improvisation

Small groups/whole group   10 mins

Objective: To show an ability to sustain a dramatic role.

The most effective way of achieving a felt sense of grievance here would be to use the *teacher-in-role* device. This allows you to help students build their role from within the drama by injecting information and asking questions in a clearly defined framework:

> You, man, come here. Take your cap off and tell me, how much of this stretch have you managed to repair today? . . . Are they the best rocks you can find? Where are you getting them from? . . . That donkey looks as if it's seen better days. Is it yours? What do you normally use it for?

The scene could end with the Chairman informing the workers that they must give another day's labour. You may then drop the role and recap on what has happened in the scene, before going on to ask the students to decide what they think should happen next.

DEVELOPMENT

Having watched some of the different scenes, you may use a form of *forum theatre* to explore further how the Chairman or other Trustees would react. For example, one group shows how the men decide to leave the work and return to their own homes. Ask volunteers to enact a scene in which some of the Trustees meet with some of the men. The rest of the class are at liberty to stop the scene and give individual players secret advice as to how to proceed.

3 Presentation/Display

Groups: 2–4

This is a flexible task which may be set as homework or developed by small groups over a short period. By placing the rest of the class in the role of the Turnpike Trust, you are providing students with a firm set of criteria by which to evaluate the work produced and mitigating the effect of any negative comments about the ideas or the presentation.

Trains And Boats And Planes (pp. 41–4)

1 and 2 Thought-Tracking/Improvisation

Groups: 2–6   5 mins

Objectives: To speculate on the meaning of a visual image.

To adopt a dramatic character and express an appropriate viewpoint.

Asking the groups to start with a tableau, and focusing on just one line of thought, gives students a secure foundation upon which to develop a dramatic character. Having asked a few members of the class to speak their thoughts aloud, you may choose simply to ask all of the group to bring the scene alive and to improvise the rest of the conversation.

DEVELOPMENT

Task **2(b)** provides the class with an opportunity to develop their characters and understanding of the historical/social changes through a piece of prepared improvisation.

3 Tableau

Groups: 3–5   15 mins

Objective: To show an understanding of how Drama may relate to other arts.

The exercise requires the students to be selective in their choice of visual and aural imagery. The objective may be met by asking them to research appropriate music or pieces of visual art to provide a background for their tableaux.

4 and 5 Improvisation

Pairs   10 mins

Objective: To identify some of the elements which make up Drama.

The nub of this exercise is that a piece of drama generally requires some form of conflict to occur. This conflict gives an improvisation a focus, if not a resolution.

DEVELOPMENT

Task **5** highlights a different sort of conflict, that is between a character and his or her own situation. In some cases, the changing situation may provide a resolution to a conflict (for example, the builder who now finds work on the canal).

6 Creative Writing

7 Discursive Writing/Meeting

Whole class   30 mins

Objective: To sustain a dramatic character and communicate an appropriate

viewpoint.

As a precursor to the meeting, invite students to find potential allies in the room without openly declaring their own standpoint and risking conflict. This requires quite sophisticated verbal skill and the ability to interpret what someone else is saying. You could adopt the role of chairperson in order to focus and control the meeting, once it looks as if students have gravitated into their own support groups.

Turnpikes And Their Keepers (pp. 46–9)

I Game

Whole group   15 mins

Objective: To use careful research to support a dramatic character.

This is a variation on a common improvisation game. The key to it is that, while accepting the truth of the dramatic situation, one of the characters continually tries to 'block' the other. For an entertaining and enlightening review of this skill, see Keith Johnstone's *Impro* (Methuen, 1981).

2 Improvisation

Pairs   10 mins

Objective: To adopt and sustain a dramatic character based on researched evidence.

3 Improvisation

Groups: 4–6   20 mins

Objective: To show a practical understanding of the importance of timing.

This is an exercise in comic timing inspired by Bob Newhart's sketch about a school which trains bus drivers in unhelpfulness!

4 Tableau

Groups: 4–6   20 mins

Objective: To use visual imagery to convey a narrative.

In contrast to the last exercise, this task requires students to look for evidence in the text which demonstrates a more sympathetic regard for the real situation of the turnpike-keepers. Following a sharing of the work, a discussion might focus on why people like the turnpike-keepers were popular targets for abuse. Are there modern comparisons (for example, traffic wardens)?

5 Creative Writing

Local Customs (pp. 51–3)

I and 2 Ritual

Groups: 4–6   20 mins

Objective: To relate a dramatic style to a broader historical and cultural context.

There are many links between what we would now recognise as a piece of drama and many social or religious rituals. Take the example of a wedding ceremony:

- the participants may wear a special costume;
- there is a given order of events;
- there is an audience;
- there is a defined space in which the event takes place.

Some rituals or celebrations still exist, although a modern audience might not understand their meaning and purpose. A useful book outlining these links further is *Mask and Scene* by Diana Devlin (Macmillan, 1989).

3 Improvisation

Whole group   20 mins

Objective: To develop ideas about the content of a drama through appropriate
            discussion and rehearsal.

Encourage students to ensure they are fulfilling the three listed requirements of the
task in order to keep the work focused and economical.

DEVELOPMENT

Task **3(b)** offers the opportunity to develop the situation through design or creative
writing. The work would lend itself to exploration through *rolling role*. Using this
technique, the class could be divided into three groups representing:

- the villagers;
- the authorities who wish to ban the custom;
- the press.

The work of each group is presented to the others who then create a written or
dramatic response, for example:

- the villagers demonstrate their custom;
- the press report on the trouble the custom generates;
- the authorities respond with a poster banning it;
- the villagers present a scene in which they decide to refuse to pay their council tax
  in protest.

4 Movement

Groups: 2–4   15 mins

Objective: To extend skill in the use of a variety of dramatic forms.

Encourage students to draw on their own knowledge of playground rhymes and
skipping games to create a new rhyme of their own.

Gypsies (pp. 56–60)

1(a) Brainstorming

Whole group   5 mins

Objective: To pool knowledge, ideas and attitudes for further discussion.

The purpose of this exercise – to recognise the whole range of attitudes and myths
about travellers – requires a 'no holds barred' policy. It is very likely, for example,
that words such as '*thieves*' and '*dirty*' will appear. A way of introducing the
activity which will dismantle some of the students' inhibitions, is to explain to the
class that whatever is recorded does not have to represent what they personally
believe, but what they suspect or know others to believe. It is essential that the class
understand that all comments will be treated seriously in discussion. Many schools
have traveller children on their roll. Rather than avoiding this type of exercise, the
sensitive teacher may use it to support those children and give them the opportunity
to dispel some of the myths which surround the travellers' way of life.

1(b) Discussion

Whole group   15 mins

Objective: To recognise the way in which myths and attitudes may be reinforced
by the media.

In chairing the discussion, try to steer students away from the anecdotal in favour
of summarising the ways in which knowledge and attitudes are acquired: personal
experience, secondhand experience, books, films, etc. Focus on any contradictions
there may be: for example, the popular media image of a gypsy may be someone
who wears a headscarf and plays the violin, but does this match the experience of
any students who have met gypsies or travellers?

2 Creative Writing

Individuals

You may choose to discuss the character of this woman's face in the light of the
previous discussion. What contradictions are implied between how the woman
looks and some of the words on the sheet of paper? Are there any words which
seem to be reflected in the look of her face?

3 Thought-Tracking

Whole group   10 mins

Objective: To adopt a dramatic character with an attitude appropriate to the given
situation.

Ask the class to decide on three simple facts about themselves as members of this
group of modern gypsies.

Are they young or old? Are they related to the dying woman or not? Do they
believe in traditional ways or do they feel that the group needs to keep up with
modern trends?

When students have decided on the cornerstones of their characters, ask individuals
to speak aloud their answers to the questions in the Students' Book and give reasons
for their replies.

DEVELOPMENT

Ask the students to write down a brief description of their character and his or her
attitudes, based on their answers to the above. They will need these descriptions in
tasks **5** and **6**.

4(a) and 4(b) Creating Characters

Whole group   10 mins

Objective: To contribute ideas for further development appropriate to an
established content.

For the purpose of the drama, the group needs to share certain key points about the
characters at the centre. One way of doing this would be to lay out the large
drawing of the rawni on the floor and place a sheet of card at each corner to
represent the four characters in the cameos. Ask the class to add simple but

important details about each cameo. As with any idea-gathering exercise, the ideas must be coherent and acceptable to the group. A common problem is that the characters become bland and stereotypical. Talk about this with the group and negotiate what apparent contradictions are acceptable and what are not. For example, stating that the young girl is a convicted mass murderer will be very difficult to accommodate in the drama; stating that she is exceptionally good in school may be justified and add an interesting potential conflict (is it right to keep moving her on?).

DEVELOPMENT

Task **4(b)** will help the class consolidate and develop the information generated through the task above.

4(c) Improvisation
Groups: 4–8   20 mins
Objective: To use a variety of dramatic forms to communicate an idea.

Encourage the class to experiment with ways of making it clear that the scene is a memory. This might require using narration or perhaps manipulating the use of space, voice and movement to signify a change in the time setting.

5 and 6 Imaging
Whole group/small groups   15 mins
Objective: To consider the importance of space and timing in dramatic
                    presentation.

Ask the class to remind themselves of the characters created in task **3** (four members of the group should represent the characters depicted in the cameos and developed in tasks **4(a)**, **(b)** and **(c)**).

- The class imagine that the outline of the woman on the floor represents her body in the old caravan. Considering their relationship and attitude, how might they stand or sit in the space surrounding the woman? Invite the class to speak aloud their thoughts again and record the different ideas.
- Ask the students, out of role now, to consider if any of the thoughts they have heard might be given more effect by putting them into a particular order; perhaps, for example, one student has offered a line which would be particularly powerful if it came last.

Try the sequence out again, asking the students to be more conscious this time of their timing, volume, tone of voice, etc. Would any carefully chosen movements add to the power of the image?

DEVELOPMENT

You might introduce task **6** in role as a police officer, entering directly after the sequence above. The improvisation might spontaneously develop into a powerful exposition of different characters and attitudes and suggest a number of interesting possible developments which can then be explored further through small group work.

7 Imaging

Groups: 4–6   15 mins

Objective: To adapt performances to suit different material.

Encourage the class to experiment with sound, movement and style. If students wish to use the spoken word, encourage them to be economical or to find alternatives to simple naturalistic dialogue. For example, they may use contrasting sequences of words from the original brainstorm, speaking them in a rhythm and repeating some for emphasis.

DEVELOPMENT

What would be an appropriate way for the students to record their images? Would it be possible to use a descriptive stage direction and written dialogue, or would some other form of notation be more helpful?

8 Creative Writing

Individuals

This task might be used to develop the last exercise. Clearly, newspaper articles, poems or stories might be produced, but some students may prefer to experiment with ordering key words into shapes or patterns, or to combine them with visual images to create a montage which reflects the relationship of the travellers to the Gaujo society.

Footpads And Canting Crews (pp. 63–5)

1–3 Knowledge About Language

These three exercises contain possibilities for creative writing, improvisation and presentation. At the heart of each is an exposure to Non-Standard, pre-twentieth-century English. Take the opportunity to discuss the fluid nature of language by asking for even more modern or local equivalents of some of these words and phrases. For example, *click* meant to steal. What word do the students use now – nick, half inch (pinch), rob?

Misery And Hazard (pp. 65–7)

1 Creative Writing

As an introduction to this task, you may wish to read and discuss the extract from Susan Hill's popular novel *The Woman in Black*, shown opposite.

2 Narration/Tableau

Groups: 3–6   20 mins

Objective: To use a variety of dramatic forms to communicate an idea.

Clearly, this task could be used by an individual as the basis for a piece of creative writing. A practical alternative would be to ask groups to formulate six key moments in the heroine's memory of the incident. While some of the group provide a tableau depicting each visual memory, she provides a narration which

That walk back was a nightmare. I was obliged to go step by slow step, for fear of veering off onto the marsh, and then into the rising water. If I looked up or around me, I was at once baffled by the moving, shifting mist, and so on I stumbled, praying to reach the house, which was farther away than I had imagined. Then, somewhere away in the swirling mist and dark, I heard the sound that lifted my heart, the distant but unmistakable clip-clop of the pony's hooves and the rumble and creak of the trap. [. . .] I stopped and waited to see a lantern – for surely he must carry one – and half wondered whether to shout and make my presence known, in case he came suddenly upon me and ran me down into the ditch.

Then I realized that the mist played tricks with sound as well as sight, for not only did the noise of the trap stay further away from me for longer than I might have expected but also it seemed to come not from directly behind me, straight down the causeway path, but instead to be away to my right, out on the marsh. I tried to work out the direction of the wind but there was none. I turned around but then the sound began to recede further away again. Baffled, I stood and waited, straining to listen through the mist. What I heard next chilled and horrified me, even though I could neither understand nor account for it. The noise of the pony trap grew fainter and then stopped abruptly and away on the marsh was a curious draining, sucking, churning sound, which went on, together with the shrill neighing and whinnying of a horse in panic, and then I heard another cry, a shout, a terrified sobbing – it was hard to decipher – but with horror I realized that it came from a child, a young child. I stood absolutely helpless in the mist that clouded me and everything from my sight, almost weeping in an agony of fear and frustration, and I know that I was hearing, beyond any doubt, appalling last noises of a pony and trap, carrying a child in it, as well as whatever adult was driving and was even now struggling desperately. It had somehow lost the causeway path and fallen into the marsh and was being dragged under by the quicksand and the pull of the incoming tide.

I began to yell until I thought my lungs would burst, and then to run forward, but then stopped, for I could see nothing and what use would that be? I could not get onto the marsh and even if I could there was no chance of my finding the pony trap or of helping its occupants, I would only, in all likelihood, risk being sucked into the marsh myself.

(from *The Woman in Black* by Susan Hill)

adds detail and links the tableaux together. Encourage the class to try and adapt the style used for the journal entries in the Students' Book. The best students will be able to include elements of gentle humour in their description of the disaster and illustrate that they have assimilated something of the idea of the romantic heroine.

3 Improvisation

Groups: 4–6 10 mins

Objective: To employ vocal and movement skills to portray a dramatic situation.

One way of setting this task would be to ask the students to improvise it spontaneously in their groups, feeding in the idea that the coach is in fact moving. Refer to the descriptions of the conditions for 'outsides' in the Students' Book and ask students to try and reflect these in their movements and voices during the scene.

4 Creative Writing

A copy of 'The Diverting History of John Gilpin' may be found in *Touchstones 1* by Michael and Peter Benton (Hodder & Stoughton, 1968). The poem lends itself to recording, with lots of possibilities for comic sound effects.

A Smuggler's Tale (pp. 70–72)

I Presentation

Groups: 4–6   30 mins

Objective: To adapt a performance to suit non-dramatic material, using a variety of dramatic techniques.

Comments on approaches to choral speech and the dramatic realisation of poetry are made on p. 85 in relation to Alfred Noyes' poem, 'The Highwayman'.

2 Evidencing

Individuals   5 mins

Objective: To find an appropriate way of recording a dramatic idea.

A variation on the usual approach to 'evidencing' would be to ask the students to consider how they have dialogues with themselves and then ask them to quickly write a page in that style, for example:

> *'What's that noise?'*
> *'It's nothing. Go to sleep.'*
> *'I'm sure I heard something. Something downstairs.'*
> *'It's your imagination. Forget it.'*
> *'Then why are there lights moving across the ceiling?'*
> *'It's just a reflection of the moonlight.'*
> *'Then why is it flashing?'*

DEVELOPMENT

Students swap their pages of dialogue with others in the group, then, in pairs, find a way of delivering the scripts as if they were two parts of one person's mind. Encourage them to make any alterations which they think would make the piece more appropriate to the period.

3 Improvisation

Groups: 2–4   20 mins

Objective: To match the style and content of a presentation to an historical and cultural context.

Groups are unlikely to have any trouble finding a modern equivalent to 'brandy-wine' as an illegal substance. Employing appropriate language and gesture to reflect the two periods is a more challenging element of the task.

DEVELOPMENT

In addition to the discussion suggested in the Students' Book about changing attitudes, some of the scenes shared may lend themselves to further exploration through *forum theatre*. For example:

- One group depicts a scene in which a young boy is caught by a drug dealer in the basement of his uncle's house. The dealer is preparing to kill the boy when the uncle enters.

  The class divide into three, each group representing one of the different characters. The groups are given a few minutes to consider what their character believes to be:
  - the worst thing that could happen as a result of the scene;
  - the best thing that could happen.

- Each group elects one person to play out the scene while the rest watch carefully. At any time, if the group thinks the player is heading towards the worst thing possible, members call 'time out'. The scene is stopped, and all of the groups may advise their player on how best to proceed.

  You may need to intervene in order to summarise the situation and discuss what would make the most satisfactory conclusion:
  - in real life;
  - in a piece of drama.

4 Interview
Whole group   30 mins
Objective: To formulate and ask questions appropriate to situation and character.

You may choose to organise this activity as pair or small group work. Students are likely to benefit from being given some time to formulate their questions and discuss the implications of the answers they receive. To promote this, you may ask them to work in small groups to prepare two questions they would like to ask each character. After this, adopt the role of each character in turn and field the questions from the class, collectively in the role of the Bow Street Runners. After each interview, the groups will need to consider the extent to which the answers match what they have understood from the journal.

5 Reportage

6 Journal

Local Legends (pp. 72–3)

I Creative Writing

2 Storyboards
Individuals/pairs
Objective: To select and order key moments in a narrative.

One of the strengths of the cartoon format is that a reader/audience can comprehend what a character in the story is thinking as well as what he or she is saying. In Drama, this involves either highly skilful manipulation of naturalistic writing and acting, or a willingness to use conventions such as the aside or other 'alienation' techniques. Students in this age group can understand, and are interested in, finding alternatives to *Neighbours*-style naturalism, even if lectures on Brecht may be inappropriate at Key Stage 3. Any opportunities teachers have to discuss the dramatic equivalents of comic strips (which are not at all alien to young people) can only broaden students' understanding of the eclecticism of Drama.

3 Creative Writing/Improvisation
Groups: 3–5   20 mins
Objective: To match ideas about content to form.

The story of the Moonrakers, like that of The Wise Men of Gotham, relies on one of the essential elements of comedy: the little person winning out over someone who is richer or more powerful. As a precursor to the work, ask the class if they can think of any examples from their own TV viewing or reading.

Crossroads (p.73)

1 Imaging
Whole group/small groups   10 mins
Objective: To consider different ways of developing a drama by focusing on the
                 choices available to one character.

An interesting development of this task which we enjoyed involved laying out two large sheets of newsprint in the form of a crossroads. A group was 'stationed' at the end of each road and asked to consider the advice it would give to the heroine. The teacher (as the heroine) then took up the position at the centre of the crossroads. Each group took turns to issue its advice as if it were a lure and the 'heroine' responded by moving down the road according to how persuasive she felt the argument was (a bit like a physical 'clap–o–meter!').

DEVELOPMENT

The groups were then invited to improvise a scene depicting the heroine's life in ten years' time, if she were to walk down that particular road. Having worked out the end product, they drew and annotated pictures along the road to mark the major events Our Heroine would have experienced along the way.

2 Analogy
Individuals/small groups

Introducing the idea of analogy (or 'brotherhoods', as Dorothy Heathcote has termed them) encourages students to make links between the work focused on in the Drama or English lesson and the rest of their personal or received experience. Inviting young people to make links of their own is a crucial element of any educational experience.

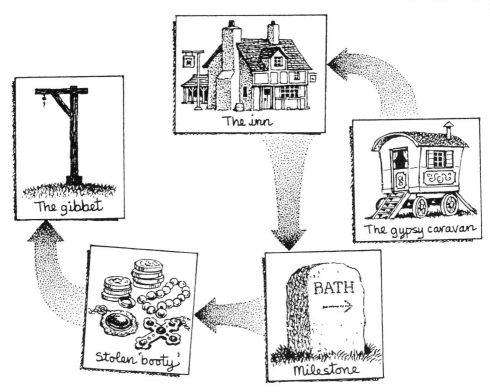

3 Personal Writing

As with other written tasks in this book, the purpose here is not so much to impart or reinforce conventional forms but rather to invite experimentation for which there may be no existing models.

Journey's End (p.75)

I Character Study

The outline below may be blown up and used as a template. This exercise involves both a sound comprehension of the entire journal and the ability to speculate on the implications of the events for the protagonist.

DEVELOPMENT

Building up from the exterior features of Our Heroine allows you to introduce the idea that an audience would learn a great deal about this character from the costume and props she uses. This raises the question of how a change or development in a character would be clearly signified.

2 Improvisation

Groups: 3   15 mins

Objectives: To introduce the 'aside' and link a particular dramatic style to an historical period.

Students will probably already be familiar with the idea of *thought-tracking*, that is speaking aloud what a character might be inwardly thinking and feeling at any given moment. Eighteenth-century English theatre made extensive comic use of the aside.

Having introduced the class to the convention, explain that this exercise makes the device even more obvious by having two actresses play the 'inner' and 'outer' personality of Our Heroine.

3 Telegram

Individuals   20 mins

Objective: To use language economically to convey a message appropriate to a
        given dramatic character.

Given the style used in the journal and any other knowledge the students have of the social conventions of the period, how might Our Heroine choose her words to make her meaning clear while remaining 'proper'? Some students may wish to share their messages, making the actual meaning of the chosen words clearer through the method of delivery.

4 Improvisation

Groups: 2–6   20 mins

Objective: To demonstrate some knowledge of the technical aspects of Drama.

Beyond the content of this improvisation, which will rely on a comprehension of the text, is the problem of how to represent a dream. If lighting is available, encourage the class to select two colours – one to represent reality and one to represent the dream. Similarly, if musical instruments are readily available, ask the groups to select one sort of sound which would signify the shift from reality to dream.

After the groups have shared their work, discuss their choices. To what extent do they think they have used conventions seen on TV/film or at the theatre?

5 Creative Writing/Improvisation

Place Names (pp. 75–6)

1 Knowledge About Language

2 Improvisation

Groups: 3   5–40 mins

Objective: To develop a piece of drama using language appropriate to the task.

This task may be tackled simply as a spontaneous improvisation. Alternatively, the class might read through the following extract from Oliver Goldsmith's *She Stoops to Conquer*, in which Tony Lumpkin is deliberately directing Hastings and Marlow astray in revenge for their insults. The groups could then devise a more polished piece of improvisation in the same style.

TONY   It's a damned long, dark, boggy, dirty, dangerous way. Stingo, tell the
               gentlemen the way to Mr Hardcastle's. (*Winking upon the Landlord.*)
               Mr Hardcastle's of Quagmire Marsh, you understand me.

LANDLORD	Master Hardcastle's! Lock-a-daisy, my masters, you're come a deadly deal wrong! When you came to the bottom of the hill, you should have crossed down Squash Lane.
MARLOW	Cross down Squash Lane!
LANDLORD	Then you were to keep straight forward, until you came to four roads.
MARLOW	Come to where four roads meet!
TONY	Ay, but you must be sure to take only one of them.
MARLOW	O, sir, you're facetious!
TONY	Then, keeping to the right, you are to go sideways till you come upon Crack-skull common: there you must look sharp for the track of the wheel, and go forward, till you come to Farmer Murrain's barn. Coming to the farmer's barn, you are to turn to the right, and then to the left, and then to the right about again, till you find the old mill.
MARLOW	Zounds, man! we could as soon find out the longitude!
HASTINGS	What's to be done, Marlow?
MARLOW	This house promises but a poor reception; though perhaps the landlord can accommodate us.
LANDLORD	Alack, master, we have but one spare bed in the whole house.
TONY	And to my knowledge, that's taken up by three lodgers already.

FURTHER READING

Novels

The Driftway	Penelope Lively (Puffin Books)
Astercote	Penelope Lively (Puffin Books)
The Revenge of Samuel Stokes	Penelope Lively (Puffin Books)
The Woman in Black	Susan Hill (Penguin Books)
Northanger Abbey	Jane Austen (Penguin Classics)
Pickwick Papers	Charles Dickens (Penguin Classics)
Gentleman Jim	Raymond Briggs (Hamish Hamilton)
The Devil on the Road	Robert Westall (Puffin Books)
Diddakoi	Rumer Godden (Puffin Books)
The Serpent's Tooth	Robert Swindells (Puffin Books)
The Ruby in the Smoke	Philip Pullman (Puffin Books)

Plays

Moll Flanders	Clare Luckham (Thomas Nelson and Sons Ltd)

Non-fiction

The Great Road to Bath	Daphne Philips (Countryside Books)
The Coaching Life	Harry Hanson (Manchester University Press, 1983)
An Old Coachman's Chatter	(EP Publishing, 1974)

CHAPTER 7: A SOUTH AFRICAN SCRAPBOOK

INTRODUCTION

Our intention in *A South African Scrapbook* has been to focus not so much on the party political conflicts of Apartheid, but on the effects of those policies upon human beings. In preparing these resources, we quickly came to the conclusion that merely to communicate the view that Apartheid is wrong, unjust and essentially insidious is too easy, too general and too simplistic. We were more concerned with the real influence of a system upon real human beings: what is the human cost?

Consequently, this is a family story, which illustrates the effect of certain ideologies on ordinary people. We would like to think of the material as a human story and, in this sense, it provides the essence of dramatic enquiry suitable for all.

The Students' Book resource material is linked by a fictional narrative – the Mathabe family story of four generations – in the form of a family scrapbook. This narrative frame is fictional, but it encompasses resources drawn together from documented factual material and extracts from South African literature.

Structures

As with the other books in the series, we propose three drama structures which link the resources in different ways and allow the students to explore the material along three different narrative paths. The structures are as follows.

A Broken Homes (The experience of the migrant worker)
The students are invited to consider the factors which might encourage young males to leave the nuclear family unit for a new life working in the compounds, and to explore the implications of such a decision upon the family which would be left behind. The work also offers the opportunity for the students to consider the cultural differences which the workers faced in the new industrial environment.

B Collision of Cultures (The white protest)
In order to challenge simplistic stereotypes of white South Africans, this structure allows the students to take the role of those white South Africans who are sympathetic to the black cause, and to explore the dilemmas and contradictions within the white society which such a position may pose.

C Reporting Apartheid
The students are encouraged to confront one of the most pertinent questions which has faced the world's press over the reporting of South Africa: how are such

emotive events to be mediated to readers in clear, impartial language, and how is this to be done in the face of an effective media ban? In the role of correspondents, the students are encouraged to explore some of the difficulties facing foreign journalists, through their efforts to report on everyday life in the townships.

In addition, there are detailed notes on all the tasks which highlight the objectives, management and structure of each activity.

STRUCTURE A: BROKEN HOMES

Aims:

- To consider the cultural differences between the village and the city, as experienced by migrant workers.
- To develop the oral and written skills to communicate this cultural experience to a given audience.
- To consider the implications for the whole family of losing a member to the city as a migrant worker.

1 Gather the class together in role as African villagers from a rural homeland. In role as the village elder, inform the students that a Government official is to visit the village the next day and that everybody must be there to meet him. As it is important to build the right context here, this opening address could indicate that nobody will be able to plough the fields, the cattle will have to be left, no work can be done on the village huts. The class need to establish a strong sense of a poor, rural, agrarian tribal community. Pairs or small groups could be asked to show, in *mime*, their everyday tasks and responsibilities, crafts or recreation.

   The students should be reminded that, as a result of the last official's visit, the Hut Tax was increased, and so attempts ought to be made on their part to welcome and pacify the visitor.

2 In a period of *dramatic play*, the villagers return in small groups to their family huts, to discuss ways in which the official can be welcomed. Why do they think he is coming?

3 It is the following day. In role as the official, gather the students together and address the village group. You have two pieces of news:
   - taxes are to increase by 10 per cent for the coming year;
   - for those who cannot afford the increase, there are jobs available in the city of Johannesburg for young, strong males.

   A decision must be made by tomorrow.

   Invite questions from the students. Remember that the jobs are not being offered by the Government, but that the official has simply heard of opportunities in factories and workplaces in the city.

4 The students return to their family groups to discuss the news. Healthy males of workable age have to be foregrounded and asked whether or not they wish to leave for work. The families can *improvise* the discussion.

5 The eldest male in each family group remembers when he left the village to go and work in the old compounds at the turn of the century. Using the 'Notice to Strong Boys' (Students' Book, p.19) as a starting point, the old man *narrates* his experiences in the compounds. He may even have been involved in the strike with Albert. Can he use his story to put the youngsters off? These stories could be *dramatised* by each small group in a short scene (the songs on pp. 16–18 of the Students' Book could be used to prepare for this) and presented to the whole class as a warning of what the future might hold.

6 In role as the official, return and gather the villagers together. Announce that, in a vote, the vast majority of all the males wish to take up the offer. Send the villagers back into their family groups. After a short *improvisation* in which the decision is discussed, settle the groups to some quiet, reflective writing.

The children can write in their schoolbooks about the things they will be able to enjoy when the wages arrive; the wives can record in diaries their fears about bringing up the family alone; the grandparents, in their diaries, may remember what it was like when the grandfathers left, and may wonder how they will cope with the increased work they will face on the farms.

7 All students now adopt the role of the migrant workers who are to leave the village. For those who have to switch roles in this way during the drama, sensitivity is needed to ensure that:
  – the students are fully aware of the nature of the new role;
  – full commitment to the new role has been established.

In order to achieve this, the first task all the workers should complete is to update their Pass Books. Using the photo of the Pass Book (Students' Book, p.46) for reference, the workers will need to manufacture a document giving personal details, including tribe, nature of last job, reasons for travelling to the new area. These documents will need to be 'stamped' and endorsed by you, as the official, before the journey can be made.

8 Set up a role play of arrival at the city railway station, using the photo on p.42 of the Students' Book. In pairs, one student can interview another using the Pass: where is he or she going? Where is he or she staying? Who gave permission for the journey? The roles can then be reversed, and the second Pass can be 'checked'.

9 Use the extract about 'the rush hour train' (Students' Book, pp. 42–3), as a stimulus for the next stage of the migrant workers' journey. In role as the township labour official, inform the workers that they are to be taken to a township hostel where they will be accommodated while jobs are organised for them. They are to travel on this train. Out of role, ask the students to prepare a *tableau* of part of the train – what was it like inside the carriages? A *soundscape* can be built up to accompany the tableau, using noises which the students think would be appropriate on such a journey. Allow the passengers to speak their thoughts aloud and in turn.

10 At the hostel, in a short period of *dramatic play*, ask the students to explore their accommodation in pairs. What do they discover? Bring them together as a whole group, and ask them to share their findings in order to build up the picture of a township hostel for migrant workers.

It is important to build a corporate picture of the hostel. If one pair suggests that it has a heated swimming pool and sauna, a free bar, or a video gamesroom, refer the matter back to the class and, out of role, ask if the suggestion is acceptable. The good sense of the whole group will usually reject any suggestions which seem inappropriate or included merely 'for a laugh'.

11 Refer the class to the photographs of 'The Rush Hour Train' and 'The Pass Check' on pp. 42 and 46 of the Students' Book. Ask the 'workers' to write their first letter home, including their experiences and feelings so far.

12 After their first week at work, the workers are given a day off to go and shop in the city, for presents to take home. The photographs of 'Separate Amenities' and 'Apartheid Signs' (pp. 55 and 56 of the Students' Book) provide images of what they may encounter (much of it unfamiliar) in this predominantly white world. In small group *improvisations*, ask the students to create scenes in which the unassuming workers break the rules set by the Apartheid signs. The scenes should show how the white citizens respond to the black people breaking these rules.

13 On their way home from the shopping trip, the workers witness the incident described in Katse's diary (Students' Book, p.44). Again in small groups, let the students act out the events of this scene. Develop the action by showing how the migrant workers (who are perhaps equally confused as to how the system works) react to the situation.

14 The photograph of 'The Clarkes' House' (p.53 of the Students' Book) would make a fitting postcard for the workers to send home to their families. How would the workers describe such a bewildering place as the city to people who have never seen anything like it?

15 One night after a long shift, and a long journey to and from work, small groups of workers gather in the hostel to share stories of their day. Using *narration*, the workers can take it in turns to describe their jobs, their places of work and their employees. (There is an opportunity here for some oral comprehension work. What kinds of jobs would these people be able to do? What would they be offered in a predominantly white business city? What are their frustrations and anxieties about working so far away from home?)

You could start this activity by *hot-seating* a confident student in role, and by letting the rest of the group question him or her about working in the city.

16 Ask the students (in small groups) to think what the workers might have dreamed about that night following the storytelling. Each group should prepare a scene which would depict the events of the dream. Is it one of longing for the family? Jealousy of the riches in the town? Or perhaps a desire to avenge some injustice at their place of work? The dreams should be presented to the rest of the class.

17 The day after the storytelling, address the group in the role of the labour official. There has been a bad accident, and one of the commuter trains has crashed. There have been many casualties; some workers have been killed. The group may wish to know more. *Hot-seat* some students in the role of those workers who travelled on the train. What was it like? Was there anything they saw which could explain the crash?

You could play Devil's advocate here and suggest that it was the workers' fault, since, because of the overcrowding, the drivers could not see clearly. The photograph of 'The Rush Hour Train' (Students' Book, p.42) could be used as evidence here. Why do the workers insist on overcrowding trains in this way?

Inform the workers that no trains will be running today. They will either have to walk to the city, or lose a day's pay. Let them work in small groups to decide what they want to do about the situation.

18 If the idea of a protest march does not emerge from one of the small group discussions, plant it yourself, in role as a subversive worker. In role, gather the group together and encourage it to plan what will be an illegal protest march. Before the march, the workers will need to *brainstorm* their grievances and their demands, and to put them in rank order. These could be painted on placards before the march takes place.

19 Lead the march to the railway offices. In a series of *paired improvisations*, the workers are given five minutes only to put their case to a transport official. How are the demands received? One or two improvisations should be presented to the rest of the group.

20 Back at the hostel, address the group, in role as a senior police officer for the township. Using *narration*, reveal to the group that the march turned into a riot on the way back to the hostel. Many arrests have been made. Tear gas had to be used, as other residents joined in. Once the idea of the drama has been instilled, invite workers to take the *hot-seat* and to explain exactly what they saw. Whose fault was it? Who started the trouble? As a representative of the police, you have the task of keeping the inquiry going by calling on participants to speak.

The meeting ends with the workers being informed that, as they have shown themselves to be troublemakers, they are to be sent back to their homelands. They will not be paid this month, as their employers have sacked them.

The workers are left to write home to their families, explaining what has happened.

21 For the workers' return, the students need to take up their original roles within the family groups. The other members of the families ask the workers why they have come back. (The letter which was completed in **20** above could be used as a point of reference here.)

In turn, the workers wants to know how the families have got on. The families could explain the hardships they have faced as a result of not having men to help with the farming. The families could act out certain incidents for the workers.

The families now need to decide whether or not they have benefited from the decision to send the workers to the city. Bring all the family groups together, and out of role, ask the class to share thoughts about the good and bad decisions the families have made. What other options were open to them? How could they have got around the increase in taxes in a different way?

STRUCTURE B: COLLISION OF CULTURES

Aims:

- To explore the experience of black women under Apartheid.
- To consider the problems facing the white 'protester'.
- To create and develop original dramatic characters, with reference to the situations outlined above in Structure A.
- To extend skills in writing in role, with an attention to context, purpose and audience.

1 If the text is available to you, read p.171 of Mark Mathabane's *Kaffir Boy* from 'What kinds of white people . . .' to 'I said, almost in tears' (the full reference for this edition is given in the bibliography on p.126). In this extract, the young Mathabane explains how he is given reading books by the white family for whom his granny works as a maid. On hearing this, his teacher dismisses the family's generosity by stating that, 'I've been in this damn world long enough to know white people inside out . . . There's no such thing as a nice white man'.

The line 'There's no such thing as a nice white man' could well introduce the theme of this structure. Draw the attention of the class to this, and ask the students to consider the following questions in pairs:

- Is it likely that all white people will support Apartheid?
- Why should the teacher make this statement?
- What difficulties do you think a white person might face if he or she opposed the system of Apartheid?

2 The class can now be arranged into small 'family' groups of four or five. These groups will adopt the roles of the white South African family around which the structure will be based. Use the photographs of 'The Clarkes' House' and 'The Clarke Family' (on pp. 53 and 54 of the Students' Book) to stimulate a short period of *dramatic play* in which the students decide on their family roles.

The groups may well need to work on each individual character. A short time should be given to *brainstorming* the background to each family member. The students will also need to decide how this family can be presented to the rest of the class: perhaps in a short scene, or through a narration delivered by the youngest member or a family friend.

3 Ask the students, in role as members of the family, to assemble around the dinner table for the evening meal. While the students *improvise* this scene, ask one of the parents from each group to come together in the middle of the space. Brief these adults on the news they have to impart to the family over dinner: the black servant has had to be sacked for unacceptable behaviour which has let the family down, and a new servant must now be sought.

The adults should now return to their respective family groups to relate the news. The family may well wish to *hot-seat* the adult (or anyone else concerned in the case) in order to find out what the 'unacceptable behaviour' was.

4 After dinner, the family discusses the appointment of the new servant. Each group, must produce:
   – a full job description;
   – a contract, with details of pay, holidays and hours;
   – an advertisement for the township newspaper.

Highlight the details here: what tasks will each individual need to have fulfilled by the servant? What will tempt the right applicant to the job, without the family having to offer more than they might consider 'worthwhile'?

5 The finished documents can now be pasted onto a wall display or blackboard, which will act as a township noticeboard. The same groups should now adopt the role of a black family in the township. In groups, allow time for the students to *brainstorm* the family relationships. The 'Township Dwelling' (Students' Book, p.41), and the description from *Kaffir Boy* of a township hut (on pp. 40–41) could be referred to in order to aid the change in imaginative focus here.

Each group sends its eldest woman of working age to the noticeboard to bring back one set of documents produced by another group. A *role play* follows in which the family discusses the pros and cons of the job. This is a real opportunity to highlight the dilemma facing the black women of the townships: their husbands' wages may well be insufficient for the family to survive on – there are most likely children to look after. What decision does the family reach?

6 The class should be split into pairs. In each pair, **A** will take the role of the woman applicant for the job, while **B** will be the family representative who will conduct the interview. Using the photo of the Pass Book (Students' Book, p.46), a Pass can be prepared showing personal details, as well as information about previous jobs and experience.

The interview can now take place in a *paired improvisation*. The interviewer will need the job description and contract in order to inform relevant questioning, and the interviewee may refer to material from the Students' Book as snapshots from the family album, which she has brought to show her new employers.

7 Announce that the appointment has now been made. The next *paired improvisation* is between the servant and a teenage member of the family. The issue here is: how would the relationship develop if the teenager were more sympathetic to the black situation?

As a whole class, share a reading of the extract from *Skin Deep* by Toeckey Jones which starts on p.36 with: 'That's something I wanted to ask –' to the end of the chapter on page 39: 'and drove home in silence' (page references are for the Pan Horizons edition, Pan Books, 1987).

As a whole class, brainstorm a character sketch of this teenager. Why is she so frustrated? What reason might she have for feeling more sympathetic to the black cause? Does she have black friends, or go to one of the new mixed schools?

If the text is not available, the following work will have to be built around a fictional character of the group's own creation. A little more time will have to be invested in the establishing of such an individual, but this is quite possible without the use of the extract from *Skin Deep*. The value in using the character of Rhonda is that, as a member of a privileged and affluent white family, she is dissatisfied with the restrictions Apartheid puts upon her life. She cannot pick her own friends, and, although she does not have any particular sympathies with the black cause, neither does she subscribe to her parents' arrogant and vociferous claims of white superiority. She is confused, and consequently depressed, because she does not fully understand her own responses to her situation.

8 In an *improvisation*, students imagine that a teenager in this situation speaks to a black servant while they are alone. Given the sympathy which the teenager has for the housemaid, what questions would he or she like to ask, and which pictures would the servant show to him or her? Use 'Albert's Letter Home' (p.25 of the Students' Book), and the 'On Tuesday' stories (p.68 of the Students' Book) as pieces of family memorabilia which the servant is prepared to share with this white teenager. What questions would the teenager like to ask about these two incidents?

9 As a response to this improvisation, the two actors can be asked to complete a piece of *writing in role*; the servant writes her first letter home, describing the house, its contents and the different members of the family; and the teenager writes in his or her diary about the character of the servant.
(This needs to be used in conjunction with 'Florence's Letter Home' on p.54 of the Students' Book.)

10 In a *small group improvisation*, the teenager is with a group of peers on the edge of the township. They come across the Bantu Warning Sign on p.39 of the Students' Book. The 'Separate Amenities' photograph on p.55 could be used as an image of what they can 'see' through the wire.

Using *thought-tracking*, the teenagers take it in turns to articulate not only what they can see, but also what that means to them in the context of their own lives as leisured white South Africans.

11 One member of each group is briefed in the following role: as a strong racist, he or she is keen to enter the township and to 'have some fun'. He or she returns to the group, and tries to encourage the others to join in. In the following *improvisation*, the teenager from the family above has the task of dissuading the group from this course of action.

12 This conflict of interests can be explored further in the following *improvisation*. In the school common room, the students sit and read the daily paper, using the article on p.48 of the Students' Book as a focus. How would the students react if they were in the school featured in the report?

A *forum theatre* could be set up for this improvisation, in which larger groups of students 'adopt' an actor from the scene and advise him or her on how to respond to the situation.

13 Back in the family home, the teenager finds the servant in tears. She has received news that her children have been involved in the township violence. (The photographs of the 'Soweto Riots' on p.63 of the Students' Book, and the 'School Protest Stories' on pp. 63–64 could be used for ideas here.) The teenager asks the servant to tell the story of her children's involvement.

14 In a *paired improvisation*, the servant asks the white woman of the house for permission to go home and see her children at this time of tension and trouble. The white woman is briefed that she has a hectic social calendar in the weeks ahead: how will she react?

The chapter 'Mma' from *Journey to Jo'Berg* (Longman edition, pp.36–39) could be used as a further example of such a situation to inform this improvisation, and, if the text is available, it could usefully be shared with the group as a stimulus.

Following the improvisations, the pairs could be given this extract as a piece of text for *performance*. How might movement, tone of voice and gesture be used to convey the status of the two characters?

15 Gather the students together in role as the 'white family' groups. In role as a white South African against Apartheid, address the class in an appeal to recruit more support for an anti-Apartheid march. How do the audience respond?

16 In a small group *role play*, the teenager (from **13** above) attends the march and afterwards takes part in a TV chat show with other whites on the question of Apartheid. The other guests need to be briefed in their roles – one has lost a

brother in a bombing raid by black campaigners, and the other is very pro-Apartheid. How does the teenager support his or her views, and what questions will the interviewer choose to ask?

17 In a follow-up *paired improvisation*, imagine the scene in which the teenager (from **16** above) returns home. The head of the family wants to know why the teenager did this against his will. As manager of the local mine, such news could affect his position. How does the conversation develop?

18 Regroup the students around the dinner table, in role again as members of the white family. On this occasion, the head of the family needs to be briefed to tell the rest of the group that, as the servant has not returned, she has been sacked. The situation is therefore as it was at the beginning of the structure.

The family is left to *improvise* the conversation which takes place about the decision to sack the servant. Is the decision a just one? Was she being neglectful of her responsibility to the family?

19 The closing activity could be a follow-up piece of *writing in role*, in which each member of the family fills out a diary entry which reveals his or her feelings about the recent events, and the sacking of the servant. These entries could be read out in turn at the dinner table as a closing *presentation*. Have any of the family members changed their views as a result of the experience?

STRUCTURE C: REPORTING APARTHEID

Aims:
- To develop spoken and written language skills, with a particular regard to context and purpose.
- To explore the notion of a personal dilemma in dramatic situations.
- To consider the consequences of free speech and of censorship.
- To create imaginative scenarios using aural images.

1 In role as a European newspaper editor, brief the class of 'journalists' on a foreign assignment you would like them to undertake. You would like them to travel to South Africa to see what living standards are really like in the townships now that the Government claims to be reforming Apartheid.

Questioning will help to settle the students into their new roles:
- Who are the reporters? Who are the photographers?
- What was their last overseas assignment? How did it go?
- Have any of them been to South Africa before? What do they know about Apartheid?
- Do they have any questions at this stage about the task ahead?

2 Using the collage of headlines on p.1 of the Students' Book, split the journalists into pairs. After reading the headlines closely, they need to make notes of all the people they would like to speak to regarding these stories. Each pair should report back to the whole group. The list of 'interviewees' the journalists are interested in can be recorded by the editor on a piece of card for later reference.

3 In role as a white South African official who is supervising the party of journalists recently arrived in South Africa, welcome them to your country and explain that you will be travelling around with them to help them find all the places that they may wish to see.

Ask questions to deepen the commitment to the roles:

- Do they have any queries about the domestic arrangements at their hotel?
- Do they have a list of any people they wish to meet?
- Where will they want to go during their visit?

Make it clear that no member of the group will be allowed to wander off alone, take pictures or conduct interviews without the permission of the guide.

4 Lead the reporters to the edge of the township. Refer them to the Bantu Warning Sign on p.39 of the Students' Book and tell them to read it before going further. Is the meaning of the sign quite clear? Use other documents in the book as stimulus for what the journalists may 'see' before them through the wire. Allow them time to inspect these pictures in pairs, commenting on what they can see, and sharing responses to the scenes.

5 Back as a group at the wire, use *thought-tracking* to allow members of the group to comment on what they can 'see'. This can be turned into a whole group presentation: ask the journalists to move slowly across the Drama space into the township, and walk among them, touching individuals on the shoulder in turn. This is the signal for students to say exactly what they can see around them, and what they are feeling about their surroundings at that particular time.

6 Split the group in half. One half will remain in role as the journalists, while the other half will adopt the role of township residents. (This latter group may need to spend time in *dramatic play* setting out a township street scene, deciding on their characters, their relationships and their occupations before the drama can develop.)

7 While the residents of the township are establishing themselves, the journalists need to plan their interviews. Refer them back to the photo on p.38 of the Students' Book. What will they want to ask about scenes such as this?

8 The reporters can now enter the township and find a resident to interview. In a series of *paired improvisations*, give the journalists time to draw out some stories about township life, and to make notes on what they discover.

9 When the interviews have run their course, the journalists can meet to prepare notes, while the group of residents, using the photograph of Joseph's classroom on p.61 of the Students' Book, recreate the detail of that room. They need to

read the picture carefully for ideas as to how large the room would be, how the students would be seated, what extra furniture there might be in the room. The group should then adopt the role of students in the class, with one volunteer as Joseph. They are discussing the events of last Tuesday, and the scene can be established through a short *improvisation*.

10 Meanwhile, show the journalists the story featured on p.64 of the Students' Book: 'Police shoot dead school protest boy'. They have the opportunity to visit the school. *Brainstorm* with them a list of information they will want to find out.

11 Let the journalists watch Joseph at work with the class for a few minutes and then, in role as the guide, interrupt the class to explain who the journalists are and what they want. In a series of *paired improvisations*, let the journalists interview a student. It may be a useful structure to impose a time limit on the interview, in order to keep a sharp focus and to stop the conversation wandering.

12 Following the paired interviews, *hot-seat* Joseph as a whole group to find out his side of the story. It may be necessary to brief Joseph on this task while the paired interviews are being conducted; no matter how strongly he may feel, he must be reminded that his words are being noted by the official and that if he says anything of which the official disapproves, his job could be in question.

This will also be an opportunity for the journalists to cross-examine Joseph about any contradictory details which have emerged from the accounts by different students – exactly what *did* happen?

13 In role as the official, suggest that in the interests of balance, the group is now to be taken to the police chief to get his side of the story. The class will now work as a whole group of journalists for the rest of the structure. In role as the chief of police, run a press conference for the journalists. They may use quotations from the school students if they wish, but a time limit ought to be set again – the police chief may well wish to leave difficult questions unanswered!

14 Break up the press conference by announcing that a large crowd is gathering to campaign against Apartheid. The police have been called to control the demonstration. Arrange the reporters at a suitable vantage point past which the marchers will have to proceed. Use the *evidencing* technique to build up a mental picture of the scene. The journalists take it in turns to say what they can 'see' (for example, a deserted street, a man putting shutters up in his windows), as well as 'hear' (the sound of distant voices, chanting and singing, police sirens, dogs barking). This is an effective way of building up an imaginative scene which the whole group can share.

A further development would be to build up gradual sound effects as the members of the class take it in turns to speak – the drum of footsteps, distant cries, swelling chants. All these can be created as a *soundscape* to accompany the spoken evidence of the scene.

15 Just as the soundscape is building to a climax and the demonstrators come into sight, address the group in role as the police chief. You announce that a ban on all reporting has been made, and that the reporters must give up their cameras, film, tape recorders and notes. Nothing can be returned. The Government does not wish this, or any other incident to be reported, and so an effective press blackout has been imposed.

16 Put the journalists into small groups and give them 60 seconds only in which to decide whether or not they wish to comply with this directive. They have this time to decide on any questions they would like to ask. Are they interested in knowing why the police will not allow filming? What do they think the police are going to do when the demonstrators arrive?

17 In a quick question-and-answer session, assess the mood of the journalists as they give their response to your demands. If they agree, they are allowed to leave without their equipment; if they do not comply, they are to be arrested.

18 The role play needs to be broken at this point: it will serve no constructive purpose simply to 'act out' a confrontation, as the drama lies in the events which create – or result from – a conflict rather than in the conflict itself. What would be far more valuable here would be a quiet, reflective period of *writing in role*. Back at the airport, waiting for a flight home, the journalists write home to their families, explaining what has happened to them, and what they have seen and, most importantly, how they feel as a result of the press ban. Emphasise that to come home from an expensive trip with nothing to show for it could mean that they lose their jobs.

19 Back in the office, address the group as an enraged editor who wants to know why they have nothing to show for their efforts, and how they came to lose all their equipment. Invite individuals to *narrate* what happened on the trip. As a follow-up, explain that they must remember a great deal of what they saw, even if they do not have the pictures. Put the journalists into small groups and ask them to create short scenes depicting one incident that each group remembers, and which they feel sums up the experience of black people under Apartheid. The scenes can be drawn from any of the situations or resources which the students have encountered in the Students' Book. These scenes can be shared as a piece of *presentation*.

20 As a follow-up task, the students can be asked to write up any of the scenes as a front page story for their newspaper back in their own country, where the ban does not apply. Which story do they wish to tell, and how is it going to be presented?

21 The paper is losing money, but has been offered a very lucrative deal from the South African Government, which is to advertise the country as a tourist attraction. It would be allowed to print this with the Government's blessing, and would be allowed to return to film the beaches, hotels and sporting facilities for the campaign. The photographs of the Clarkes' family home and the white amenities (pp. 53 and 55 of the Students' Book) could be used as exemplar material which the South Africans have proposed using. How do the journalists feel about the idea?

22 Set up an AGM at which the newspaper staff gather to decide whether or not to accept the offer. The students need to decide on roles: journalists, shareholders, printworkers, advertisers, and the editors. Each group needs to be made aware of how the plan will affect it. Make this clear in the editor's opening address, which you must give in role: if the paper goes under, all the workers will be sacked and the shareholders will lose out, but there might be a feeling of professional principle at stake for some . . .

23 *Forum theatre* would offer a valuable structure for this whole group activity. Each of the above groups of employees selects an actor to represent its views in a central role play of the meeting. At any point, the rest of the group, acting as audience, can call a 'time out', in which the improvisation is suspended for 60 seconds while the actor is briefed on how to proceed in the debate, or how to deal with difficult opponents in the discussion.

The improvisation then begins again. The meeting should have a strict time limit, after which a vote is taken by all the students.

R e s o u r c e s

These notes are offered as a guide to activities based on individual resources and give a clear suggestion as to the aim of the exercise, the recommended time to be taken, and the number of students to be involved.

The Mathabes' Story (pp. 4–5)

Discussion (Tasks 1–2)
Pairs/whole class   10 mins
Objective: To establish an understanding of the key term Apartheid, and to explore images which convey this understanding.

Be prepared to accept anything, regardless of the level of sophistication. For some students, the idea that the South Africans play rugby may, at this stage, be as significant to them as the system of Apartheid. All suggestions will help to build up a picture of the country's culture. In the same way, be ready to accept all suggestions as to how humans can be said to be 'different', even if they sound ludicrous (for example, hair colour, height, even taste in music).

Give the class time to record all the ideas onto a map of the country that you have put on the wall. You may choose to record the details of the country inside the outline, the definitions of 'separateness' outside, or to mix them all up as a collage of images.

Tableau/Improvisation (Tasks 3–5)

Groups: 3–5   15 mins

Students should concentrate here on how placing a group in relation to an individual, using positioning to convey status, and using expression to denote state of mind, can all convey meaning. What happened before, or afterwards, can then be explored in the improvisation, in which dialogue, names, relationships, etc., can be explored.

The improvisation can, of course, be completely unrelated to the tableau, but students should be given the option of using the latter as the opening for, or closing of, the former.

Village Life (pp. 11–12)

Depiction (Tasks 1–2)

Groups: 5–6   5 mins

Objective: To create dramatic characters in a given context.

The importance is to see how strong the students' visual comprehension is. Their assumed tasks need to reflect the culture depicted in the illustrations. As before, if a student offers a ridiculous suggestion (for example, 'I am mending the tribal Range Rover'), simply stop the activity and ask the whole class if they are prepared to accept the suggestion.

Improvisation (Task 3)

Groups: 5–6   5 mins

One or two students 'narrate' the sighting so that the discussion may take place. Encourage the class to consider, and propose, the options for the tribespeople, and stress that, by the end of the improvisation, a decision must have been reached.

Prediction/Narration (Tasks 4–6)

Objective: To develop skills in narration, drawing on the students' knowledge of how stories are structured.

It might help to discuss the cultural context of this story and the way this might differ from those with which students are more familiar. The moral nature of many oral narratives could also be introduced here, with reference to Aesop's fables. If this story was intended to be moralistic, what would it teach, and how?

The Family Tree (pp. 13–14)

Narration (Tasks 1–4)

Whole group   20 mins

Objective: To contribute to the presentation of oral narratives.

Organise a quick question-and-answer session to check that the relationships within Sissie's family are understood. Encourage the students to involve themselves in the deconstruction of these relationships: what do the facts tell us about the way the family lived? For example, prompt consideration of the length of life enjoyed by the different generations, the numbers of offspring, the parental age when children are born, etc. How does this compare with students' experience of their own families?

Give the research into students' own family trees high status, even though it will not be explored by the structures which follow. If possible, provide room on the display board for the students to record their research as the drama unfolds. 'Family stories' would be an interesting way to close sessions, particularly if comparison is made with the Mathabe family.

Work Songs (pp. 16–18)

Presentation (Tasks 1–3)
Pairs/groups: 4   15 mins
Objective: To explore the relationship between the appropriate form of
                     presentation for a poem, and the language of its content.

Read the poems aloud to the students before they begin work. On a simple level, what is being addressed here is the tone and mood of the poems. Encourage the students to discuss this by asking questions. How does the poem leave you feeling? Where do you get that feeling from? How will you get that feeling across to your audience?

Make copies of the poems (one for each group) for groups to annotate with suggestions for presentation. Introduce the techniques of choral reading, soundscape, use of sound effects, etc.

Notice to Strong Boys (pp. 19–20)

Discussion/Hot-Seating (Tasks 1–4)
Groups: 4   20 mins
Objective: To extend reading for understanding skills.

Once the students have read and understood this text, both its surface features and its subtext, ask them if they trust the writer of the text. *Hot-seat* a student in role as the author. This person will need to be carefully briefed; he or she clearly needs to recruit workers and so cannot tell lies, but if there are drawbacks to the work, does he or she want to make these explicit to the villagers?

The rereading of the tribal song calls for co-operative group work. The students need to pick out specific textual references which provide evidence of the reality of mine work.

Albert in the compound (pp. 20–22)

Writing In Role (Tasks 1–5)
Pairs/groups/individuals   30 mins+
Objective: To create dramatic characters with conflicting points of view to
                     facilitate writing in role.

Once the four roles (Albert's brother, the tout, Albert's wife and a young man wishing to follow Albert) have been established, give the four groups a few minutes to form and to improvise their roles. What do they think about mine work, and how do they justify their position? The writing in role could follow this 'warm-up'. The writing of the article will involve a different role again, but its strength will rely on how many of the different viewpoints the journalists can include in their copy. The in-role jottings can be used as quotations or reported speech in the final article.

Improvisation (Tasks 6–7)
Pairs/groups   15 mins

The reports from the activity above should, where possible, be used as the stimulus for this improvisation. Both roles are important to the conversation: Albert faces a dilemma as to how much of the painful truth he is going to relate, while the family member needs to be aware that problems will also have to be faced at home as a result of his absence. What is happening to the village farms now that the young men have left? How will Albert respond to this news?

Albert's Trial (pp. 26–29)

Forum Theatre (Tasks 1–2)
Whole group   25 mins
Objective: To communicate a particular viewpoint to a given audience in a
                   particular context.

Following the opening *improvisation*, all the actors playing Albert, the policeman and the observer gather into three respective groups. A volunteer is called for from each group. These actors set up the courtroom in the middle of the space while the remaining members of the group are briefed on their roles – they have the responsibility for their actor, and can call a 'time out' to advise him or her whenever a difficulty arises.

The trial is now improvised; the observer takes the role of the defence, the policeman that of the prosecution. If you consider it to be appropriate, you could take the role of the judge, whose job it will be to wind up the hearing and to pronounce a verdict.

Work Songs (pp. 27–28)

Presentation (Tasks 1–5)
Individuals/groups/pairs   15 mins
Objective: To experiment with sound and movement to convey the mood of
                   poetry.

Groups need to be briefed on how visual images as well as sounds can create mood. In answer to the question 'How do the poems leave you feeling?', the students will need to select appropriate images from the range of facial expressions, tableaux, sound effects and soundscaping they can think of to convey this feeling.

Moving House (p.35)

Role Play (Tasks 1–2)

Groups: 2–4   10 mins

Objective: To extend a dramatic character through dilemma.

The danger here is that the conversation might easily disintegrate into a violent bawling match! As the stress is on use of language, the actors must be encouraged to express their views as clearly as they can, but within the context of the improvisation. The residents are friends of the worker and so, rather than abuse him, they may well wish to appeal to communal loyalties to win him over. On the other hand, the worker has to express the desires of his employers, or his valuable job may be at risk.

Moving House (pp. 36–37)

Tableau (Tasks 1–3)

Groups: 4–5   10 mins

Objective: To develop language skills to convey and to describe what is seen, understood and felt in a specific context.

The students will need to think carefully about what kind of possessions a family
such as the one in the photograph might have owned, and which would be practical to take. (How does it look as though they are travelling?) Such attention to detail will negate insensitive suggestions such as video recorders, stereos or freezers.

Also, encourage students to describe the items rather than simply list them. What are the small, but significant details which make then unique? Are there any family stories behind the objects (for example was this item a present? How did the family come by it?). In role, the class should be encouraged to offer such anecdotes.

Poetry (Task 4)

Individuals

The written follow-up needs to take account of the sentimental value of such objects. What thoughts do these items bring to mind as they are handled in this particular context? The poems may well be about the happier times which an object brings to mind rather than a simple description of the thing itself.

Township Dwellings (pp. 39–41)

Role Play (Tasks 1–4)

Pairs   20 mins

Objective: To create an imaginative sense of place.

Students should read the photograph on a 'surface level' (what are the buildings like? How much room is there?) as well as on a deeper level. What does the wire suggest to you about the nature of the place? How would living here make you feel?

Encourage students to draw on the rest of the resource material in building an imaginative picture. When in role as the housing agent, you may also want to hint at possible areas which the group could expose in meaningful dramatic exploration. For example, how far away are the shops, parks (if any) and schools? What are these facilities like? Although not directly related to the picture, you could open up these areas by alluding to them in your address. For example, the economic laws of Apartheid meant that there are very few stores or supermarkets in the townships. The black people were not encouraged in business enterprise, and, as a result, had to shop far away in downtown white areas. The few services which were available were mainly street vendors, pavement stalls or travelling carts selling offal or poor quality meat – the only meat within the budget of many black people.

The students' dramatic exploration of the streets should not be restricted to the visual. How do the streets smell? How do they feel underfoot to the blind partner? What noises can be heard? Such sense impressions should deepen the visual details of the sighted partner.

'Meadowlands' (pp. 40–41)

Research (Tasks 1–4)
Individuals/pairs/groups   20 mins +
Objective: To establish an understanding of euphemism, and the function of this device in our language and culture.

This exercise should not be restricted to the dictionary definition of euphemism; examples should be drawn from the students' experience, if possible, to illustrate the concept. What differences are there between

– 'dustbin man' and 'refuse collector'
– 'toilet' and 'powder room'
– 'to die' and 'to pass away'?

This research could be developed by considering the names of streets and roads where the students live: why are streets on estates named after wild flowers, birds, poets or lakes?

Referring now to the resource material, why would the Government choose a name such as 'Meadowlands'? What associations does this word have for the students? What does this encourage us to think about this place?

Rush Hour Train (pp. 42–43)

Poetry Writing/Presentation (Tasks 1–3)
Groups: 2–4   30 mins +
Objective: To use a visual image as the stimulus for poetry writing.

Students may compose the poem individually or collaboratively; if collaboratively, the groups will have to select one example to present.

W. H. Auden's poem, 'Night Mail', would be a good example to use before this task to show how rhythm and metre can help to convey meaning. Rhythm and metre could also be highlighted in the oral presentation, with chants or sound effects emphasising the beat.

Katse's Diary: 18 August (pp. 44–45)

Tableau/Hot-Seating
Groups: 4   10 mins
Objective: To depict a written narrative in dramatic form.

The number of tableaux ought to be restricted to four or five; too many will result in a lack of clarity and focus. Stress the smooth movement from tableau to tableau by way of presentation. If this is done well, the change of mood and emotion in the scene will be made clear.

Improvisation (Tasks 3–4)
Pairs   5 mins

To deepen the conflict in this improvisation, the actors playing Katse need to be made aware that his failure to act positively in the interests of his white passengers has put his job in jeopardy. This will place the actor in an interesting dilemma: is he going to be honest, admit his sympathy for the black youngsters and thereby risk his job, or is he going to conceal his true feelings and make excuses?

The Pass Checks (pp. 45–52)

Improvisation (Tasks 1–2)
Pairs   10 mins
Objective: To explore the ways in which language confers power and status.

For these improvisations, students need to:
- look closely at the examples of Afrikaans given in the Students' Book;
- talk about words and phrases they use – or hear others use – which are intended to raise their status, or to make them feel 'big';
- consider the tone of address, as well as the vocabulary used.

As a precursor to this activity, give each pair a line, and see how many different tones they can use to deliver it (for example, as a chat-up line, as a command by a sergeant major, as an excuse by a guilty student, etc.). The audience may well like to reflect on the tone of delivery, and what this tells us about the speaker's state of mind.

In the following role play of the Pass Checks, the students can then consider how the words are delivered, as well as which words are chosen.

Writing The Report (Task 3)
Individuals   60 mins +

Stress the importance of note taking, or of tape recording interviews, whether hot-seating is carried out in small groups, or as a whole class. The statement may well be biased: the author has the right to display sympathy for either the runner or the police, as long as the statement contains evidence for the author's position.

The story will need rather more careful management. Where possible, language ought to be used to present a clear, unbiased account of the incident. Draw attention to the language of the media: headlines, paragraph organisation and the use of reported speech.

The Clarke Household (pp. 53–56)

Descriptive Writing (Tasks 1–5)

Pairs/individuals   30 mins

Objective: To set up a written transactional task with a clear sense of audience and purpose.

Initial discussion of the detail of the photograph is very important. Given the size of the house, the grounds and the style of the building, what possessions and furniture would students be likely to find inside?

The focus of this exercise is upon language use. How can descriptive language and selection of detail enhance a description? Some examples of estate agents' details, or house advertisements, could be provided, and the idea of euphemism revisited: what do the phrases 'mature', 'would suit the DIY enthusiast', 'full of character', 'compact' *really* mean? Are there other examples which would help the agents in their work in this exercise?

Separate Amenities (pp. 55–58)

Role Play (Tasks 1–3)

Pairs/groups: 6   10 mins

Objective: To create dramatic characters in order to explore the controversies of 'separate amenities'.

Students need to think carefully about:
– the background to their characters;
– the layout of the room in which the improvisation is to take place.

Is the conversation to take place on the veranda, over the dinner table, in some other place? Allow time for social 'chit-chat' before the issue of the separate amenities is introduced. This will help to establish characters and relationships before the conflict of viewpoints.

There will be a tension here which the actors will have to consider: how far are they prepared to risk the friendship by asserting their objections to what they have seen?

Always a Suspect (pp. 58–59)

Cloze Procedure/Presentation (Tasks 1–3)

Pairs/groups: 3–4   10 mins

Objective: To write poetry in response to the resource material.

The cloze procedure exercise has been designed to draw the students' attention to the emotive nature of some of the language in this poem. The text is included below, with the missing words.

It would be useful to discuss the words which the students suggest could fill the gaps before giving them the complete version. The key point here is that there is no right or wrong answer: the students are in a sense rewriting the poem in their own way, making a new meaning out of the existing text in the light of their own reading, and the object is not to choose exactly the same word as the poet. However, you could make the points listed here beneath the complete text when providing the missing words.

Always a Suspect

I get up in the morning
and dress up like a gentleman –
A white shirt, a tie and a suit.

I walk into the street
to be met by a man
who tells me to 'produce'.
I show him
the document of my existence,
to be scrutinised and given the nod.

Then I enter the foyer of a building
to have my way barred by a commissionaire.
'What do you want?'

    I trudge the city pavements
    side by side with madam
    who shifts her handbag
    from one side to the other,
    and looks at me with eyes that say
    'Ha! Ha! I know who you are;
    beneath those fine clothes
    ticks the heart of a thief'.
          Mbuyiseni Oswald Mtshali

Notes on 'Always a Suspect'

gentleman – gives an idea of status and importance. Do black people feel important as a matter of course? Why does this man have to dress up to feel like a gentleman?

existence – this word lays a great deal of stress on the Pass; it is as though the individual does not 'exist' without it.

scrutinised – the idea of status is evident again here. The man is inspected or checked as though he were not human – a commodity? The word also suggests a certain suspicion on behalf of the other: what reason is there for anyone to feel suspicious of this man?

trudge — a verb of action which clearly denotes a state of mind. How does this suggest the man is feeling as a result of the way he has been treated? How do the students feel when they are tempted to trudge? Compare this with other verbs (skip, stroll, march). What do these words suggest about a person's mood?

madam — a word which again conveys a strong sense of status and a corresponding humility on the speaker's behalf (refer back to language work on p.119).

eyes — this image is important as it hints at the level of non-verbal communication through which racist attitudes can also be conveyed. Body language is a powerful link in which people can be made to feel inferior.

fine — the notion of appearance is again highlighted (links back to idea of dressing like a gentleman). The point is that racist attitudes stem essentially from differences in the way we appear, rather than in what essentially we are.

thief — another extremely emotive term. What evidence is there in the poem that this man is dishonest? The only clue can be his colour – his clothes are fine. So, what is the poem suggesting about the associations some white people make with black skin colour?

Writing Poetry (Task 4)
Individuals

Although this is a fairly open brief which gives students the chance to reflect on the resource material, the subtleties of this poem should not be forgotten: racism is just as evident in a look (or a *failure* to take notice), a positioning of the body or a facial expression, as in a comment, an action or an act of violence. Students need to try to accommodate this kind of non-verbal communication in their work.

The Orlando Power Station (pp. 60–61)

Improvisation/Letter Writing (Tasks 1–3)
Pairs   30 mins +
Objective: To develop conflicting viewpoints in a dramatic and written form.

The class could first consider the implications of having no electric power. Following the *brainstorming* session, ask the students to work in pairs to think up an incident which might occur due to a lack of electricity in the township. These ideas may derive from the students' own experience, although the problems in the township will obviously be far worse. For example:
– children not being able to do homework after dark;
– journeys becoming more hazardous at night;
– a limitation of services in the event of a domestic accident.

The students may wish to decide on one such event *before* the improvisation or the letter writing. This incident would give the argument greater force and lend weight to the exchanges which follow in the next two activities.

Joseph's School (pp. 61–67)

Role Play (Task 1)
Pairs/whole group   15 mins
Objective: To create an imaginative picture of a township school.

The 'candidates' have a difficult task, in that they have to adopt not only the viewpoint of a teacher but that of a teacher in a context outside their own experience. To help them construct this role, students could consider what sort of questions a candidate might ask at their own school. Highlight the various areas of interest for a prospective employee: facilities, timetable, class size, school discipline, etc.

Do not be unduly concerned if the candidates are prone to ask questions which relate more directly to their own school experience: the answers to such questions will merely serve to highlight the gap between standards in their school and those in a poor, black township.

Letter Writing (Task 2)
Individual   30 mins +

Discuss the broader benefits of education before the students write their letters. How can a good education improve an individual's life chances; or allow a person greater autonomy?

On Tuesday (pp. 67–70)

Writing in Role/Improvisation (Tasks 1–2)
Pairs   40 mins +
Objective: To inspect a particular confrontation from the different viewpoints
               involved.

The students will need to decide on a role before attempting the anonymous statement. They may well embellish the 'facts' before them by inventing other details or events which they remember having seen. This ought to be encouraged, within the confines of this task, as it will make for a fruitful follow-up discussion on how we see things in different ways. Why is it that witnesses so often give conflicting details of an event in court, for example?

Paired Improvisation (Tasks 3–7)
Pairs   10 mins +

One way of structuring this task is as two distinct paired improvisations, in which you will have to assist the switch of roles (from police officer to student) and help the students to focus on the issue from a different point of view.

For example, you could introduce the police officer by saying:

> You have been on duty now for a long time, and you are hot and thirsty. Many officers around you are getting impatient. One of your colleagues has been taken to hospital with a cut on his head. You have seen youths throwing stones, and you are anxious to see the troublemakers brought to justice. You have been waiting patiently for a long time at the school gates, and now you can see the Principal coming out of the school . . .

And then, at the point of switching roles to that of the students:

> You have been cooped up in the classroom ever since first thing this morning, and nobody has been able to work because you are all too scared. Your friend was caught in tear gas at a disturbance last week, so you know how unpleasant the effects can be, and you have seen the police carrying tear gas cannisters today. You got to school before the trouble started but you did see some stones being thrown at the police, although not who threw them. Your brother set off for school after you did this morning, and has not yet arrived . . .

An alternative method of managing this task would be to divide the class into three groups: one group takes the role of Joseph; the other two groups take those of the police officer and student respectively. This would remove the difficulty of students having to swap roles, but would mean that one group would be acting as an audience to the other role play.

(The **staff meeting** may also provide an opportunity for *forum theatre*, as a means of developing this exercise.)

Conflict Between Walter and Joseph (pp. 70–75)

Improvisation/Hot-Seating (Tasks 1–5)
Whole group/groups   20 mins
Objective: To create dramatic characters and to inspect the effect Apartheid has
upon family relationships.

Esther's role here is key. Is she dominant or sensitive? Will her brothers listen to her, or do they tend to ignore her? Has she a special relationship with one particular brother, or does she relate to them both in the same way? Does she have a particularly strong standpoint on Apartheid?

In this three-way improvisation, there is scope for a good deal of complex debate. Although the brothers are from the same family (so conflicting tribal ties are not an issue), they may well have sympathies with the different ideological movements of ANC and Inkatha: Joseph admits to having supported rallies on behalf of the former, while Walter has made his money largely out of Zulu migrant workers who drink in his Shebeens and who traditionally support the Inkatha group. Careful reading and discussion of this material before the improvisation should increase the sophistication of the work produced.

The improvisation involving the customers provides an opportunity to explore this situation further: if the customers are predominantly Zulu tribesmen who support Inkatha, how sympathetic will they be towards students who are attacked by the police for violence in support of the ANC?

In Search of Dragon's Mountain: The Play Extract

The extract from Toeckey Jones' play, *In Search of Dragon's Mountain*, has been included for two reasons:

(*a*) the extract touches on many of the images, events and issues which have been covered in the resource material, and thus draws together the disparate experiences of the family scrapbook in a particular dramatic context; and

(*b*) by telling its story through the eyes of different generations, and hinting at the future lives of Johnnie and Temba, it builds on the narrative structure of the scrapbook and provides students with an opportunity to consider Sissie's future as a character.

The **Questions to think and talk about** have been designed to stimulate discussion of the content of the extract, and to allow students to share their understanding of what is happening. Following a whole class reading of the extract, divide the students into mixed-ability groups and ask them to discuss the questions. (A second reading of the piece in small groups may be helpful before the discussion takes place.)

A brief 'reporting back' session via an elected spokesperson from each group may be useful, but the value of the work will be in the discussion itself, not in the plenary session.

Tasks (pp. 83–84)

Tasks **1–3** relate to the performance of the extract as though in rehearsal. The students have been given the key terms of *form* and *content*, but you will need to intervene at times to reinforce these ideas. The students have the content in the script. What they are now being asked to consider is not only the 'what', but also the 'how': 'how shall we deliver our lines in performance?'

Make this distinction clear in your introduction to the tasks. The following points may also be helpful when considering where, and how, to intervene with the following group work:

(*a*) The small groups need to have at least three members, and the group members may well decide to appoint one (or two) members as director(s). Because the aim is to consider how, and not just what, is being said, the actors will need advice on how to move, speak, use the space around them, etc. (Larger groups may wish to appoint a designer, who may decide on the set for the scene, or how it might be lit.)

(*b*) The groups will also need to consider which words/lines are imporant, and need to be stressed. The directors may need help on this: actors can lay stress on words by volume, tone of voice, but also by gesture, posture and movement.

What is the effect of holding up a fist when a line is being delivered, or pointing close to someone's eyes?

(c) The word 'mood' is a complex one which may need some careful elucidation. Mood can be described as the atmosphere of the scene: its 'tonality' – a term which hints at how mood can be created, by varying the tone in which the lines are delivered. For example, the actors can be encouraged to pick a chosen line, and to deliver it in an angry voice, a depressed voice, as if they are giving the punchline of a joke, or even as if they are chatting someone up! This may well provide a good deal of fun, and it should also reveal the way in which tone of voice alone can convey meaning. (Of course, there are other means of establishing mood, and the designers mentioned above may well wish to experiment with lighting and sound to help create a mood for the scene.)

Task **4** has been included to explore the subtext of the extract – the thoughts and feelings which remain unspoken by the actors. This can be dramatised simply by allowing the actors to deliver their thoughts and feelings between lines, or to use a second actor as an 'alter ego', who can comment from another position on what the character is really feeling inside. Here, the subtext, rather than the actual text itself, is the main focus for the audience. Do they agree with how a group has interpreted the character's true feelings?

For tasks **5–7** you may need to clarify the notion of *personification* before you start. When an inanimate object is given the qualities of human life, we say it has been personified – but can the group draw examples from its own reading/ experience to highlight this?

Remind the students that, when they direct 'Apartheid' as a character in their own scenes, it is what this character *stands for* which is important, rather than his/her existence as a realistic, 'rounded' character. You need to make the same point about the creation of other personifications. If, in the final task, 'Apartheid' were to meet 'Justice', the improvisation would move away from realism into abstraction of ideas, and the stress would be on what these two had to say to each other, rather than on how they met and on what happens next. The presentation and dressing of Apartheid and Justice provide rich scope for small group work. Designs for costumes, props and make-up could all be prepared to accompany the group's practical work.

FURTHER READING

Novels

Journey to Jo'Berg	Beverly Naidoo (Longman Sky Books)
Chain of Fire	Beverly Naidoo (Longman Sky Books)
Skin Deep	Toeckey Jones (Pan Horizons, 1987)
Go Well, Stay Well	Toeckey Jones (Heinemann Windmill)

Waiting for the Rain	Sheila Gordon (Collins Cascades, 1989)
Somewhere Tenderness Survives	ed. Hazel Rochman (Collins Cascades, 1992)
Words by Heart	Ouida Sebestyen (Collins Cascades)
Cry the Beloved Country	Alan Paton (Penguin Books)
South African Stories	ed. Stephen Gray (Penguin, 1985)
African Myths and Legends	retold by Kathleen Arnott (Oxford University Press, 1989)
Comfort Herself	Geraldine Kaye (Heinemann Windmill)
Underground to Canada	Barbara Smucker (Heinemann Windmill)
My Mate Shofiq	Jan Needle (Collins Cascades)
The Friends	Rosa Guy (Penguin)

Drama

In Search of Dragon's Mountain	Toeckey Jones (Thomas Nelson and Sons Ltd)
Master Harold and The Boys	A. Fugard (Oxford University Press)
The Biko Inquest	Fenton & Blair (Rex Rollings)

Non-fiction

Apartheid: A Teacher's Guide	Godfrey N. Brown
Children Under Apartheid	IDAF
Apartheid: A History	Brian Lapping (Paladin)
Two Dogs and Freedom	Township Children (Ravan Press, 1986)
The Apartheid Handbook	Roger Ormond
Kaffir Boy	Mark Mathabane